THE

Razor and the *Mirror*

from a *child's* HEART

By
Christian-Michelle Dickerson

Published by

BUCEPHALUS Inc.

1

The Razor and the Mirror
From A Child's Heart

Is printed in The United States of America
By: www.lulu.com

Library of Congress Control Number **PBP51738**

ISBN: 978- 0- 6151 - 7893- 6

Cover Illustrations by: Muhammad Rasheed

First Published in 2006 by:

Bucephalus Inc.

Acclaim for The Razor and the Mirror

This is not a book that one sits and reads idly from page to page to page. It touches an absolute chord in the reader's mind; the plight this child endured in his daily life. A reader that possesses any compassion may experience immense difficulty reading the book because of the hurt and pain expressed by the author. There is little to no color expressed as this child managed the challenges he faced. As the book unfolds, you hope that some fraction of what is written is a lie, a mistruth some hope that this fragile little one could not have experienced the brutal acts as presented but, perhaps the child's bad dream or figment of the child's imagination.

To read the voice of the child expressed in clear, descriptive, authentic language tears at the heart, even the hardened of hearts would be moved to tears. In my experience as a counselor on child and adolescent units of two hospitals in two different states, as well as a kindergarten teacher in two different state systems, I have worked with children who have suffered chronic physical and sexual abuse usually at the hands of family members. One does not become immune after working with the children, but an overwhelming sense of helplessness where and how do we prevent the abuse?

This is a very revealing work. We are obliged to pray for the writer and those who suffer in silence. We should join the author to raise the VOICE for the least of us. *"The Razor and the Mirror"* awakens the soul.

Dr. Janice LeeNora Butler
Cumberland County School System
Fayetteville, North Carolina

"Moving, revealing and powerful! Walks Tall Wolf is on a mission from God to eradicate the pain and suffering of abuse victims. Bobby's story, *"The Razor and the Mirror,"* needs to be heard in every corner of the earth. His story is a rich and complex story that leaves the reader saddened but also hopeful. It is highly recommended to those that are empowered to become effective advocates for the sufferer."

Dr. Gigi Lamont
Social Worker/Advocate

In Memory Of:
Mr. Langston Hughes

Genius Child

This is a song for the genius child.

Sing it softly, for the song is wild.

Sing it softly, as ever you can

Lest the song get out of hand.

Nobody loves a genius child.

Can you love an Eagle,

Tame or Wild?

Wild or tame,

Can you love a monster

Of frightening name?

Nobody loves a genius child.

Kill him and let his soul run wild!

Walks Tall Wolf

You are like a shining mist that creates a star.
Only visible to the eye momentarily,
Until the collective forces creates a new one.

My prayer for you is that you know your worth,
See the beauty inside of the smile, joy, laughter,
You give to others, in turn giving back to yourself.

You walk tall even when just standing in a
stationary position.
The disposition you project is nothing short of
awesome but still friendly and warm.

I pray your heart is mended to yet love again, not
just a woman, but for yourself and the family you
are forever apart of.

Rest heavily humble wolf, for the moon yet rises for
you to adore and revere.

I know you will make it with love, because your
smile is true evidence.

In Memory Of My Friend
Brother in Arms Forever

Peter E. Gutloff
GMM3 KIA November 1969
Republic Of South Vietnam

Bobby
Brother in Arms Forever

Robert E. Dickerson
October 12, 1949 – April 18, 2003
U.S.M.C.

This Book Is Dedicated To:

For Inflicting The Pain That I Needed To Complete This Book:

Ms. Antonette Verona Douglas
Ms. Cidney Germaine Jenkins

For Joy and Happiness:

Ms. Dawn Heather Dickerson
Ms. Christian Dickerson
Ms. Bettina Paige Dickerson
Ms. Bonita Randolph

For Always Believing in Me:

Ms. Mattie T. Bailey   Mr. Robert L. Gaines Jr.
Mrs. Jessie Reed   Mr. Kevin Daniels
Mr. Booker T. Reed   Mr. M. Murray
Ms. Carolyn Green
Ms. Gertelle Doyle Padgett
Ms. Linda Day
&
Mr. Richard Manley

In Loving Memory:

PFC Adolphus M. Bailey
Mr. Eddie Lee Walker
Mrs. Margaret Beckford
Mrs. Francis Gutloff
Mr. Morgan Hampton
Mrs. Charlotte Hampton
Mr. Booker T. Reed Sr. - Mr. & Mrs. Robert L. Doyle Sr.

And to all the children who suffer in silence

About the Author

Christian-Michelle Dickerson is in Raleigh North Carolina and is homeless living on the streets of that city. Christian-Michelle spends his days talking to Skyy Joe the hot dog man, and his nights walking the streets between New Hope and New Bern because he has nowhere to sleep, no safe place to lay his head.

He is divorced and the father of two beautiful daughters. The oldest, Dawn Heather, is a graduate of Saint Paul's College where she earned her Bachelors Degree in Education. She then went on to earn two Masters Degrees at George Mason University. Christian, the youngest, resides in Annandale and is a graduate of Key Center in Springfield, Virginia.

He hails from New York City and was raised in Harlem during the turbulent years of the Civil Rights movement. There he was exposed to great men and women of color such as, Langston Hughes, who often sat with Christian-Michelle on the steps of his Harlem Brownstone and read to him, Sugar Ray Robinson, Jackie Robinson and Roy Campanella, Willie Mays played stickball with him, Etta James, James Baldwin, Claude Brown, Rose Morgan and the most honorable man that he ever met, Malcolm X, whom he saw often walking the streets of Harlem.

I thought he was the greatest thing to happen to the Black Race," Christian-Michelle once said. He went on, "After his death I could never again walk past Unity Funeral Home without remembering the horrible cold of that day I spent standing in line with hundreds of other people of color waiting to view his body." "That day was so very cold and wet." "I believe the movement became frozen in time, no more progress for men of color and the world of coloreds cried because life for people of color would never again be the same."

"It was the beginning of the Vietnam war and the end of solidarity between the races of color. "They," he stated, fought to be integrated into a white world, then separated themselves by education and class and practiced segregation among one another." "The battle had just begun, and they gave up what could have been the high ground, and lost the war." "They are, without a doubt, divided and conquered."

Forward

When I, after much deliberate consideration, decided to tell Bobby's story I wondered what the receipt of such a detailed story about a child's life would be. Those who are alive today would, more likely than not, deny any knowledge of the abuse this child endured on a daily basis.

Those who are dead may have known and participated in the inflicting of harm on the child. So I will never find out what their story is or what actions they took or could have taken to prevent the less than human treatment of an innocent child. There is not a doubt in my mind that depression was an illness Bobby was never able to overcome. Not even after he received medical treatment for this deadly mental illness.

The wounds were cut too deep. The scars were very evident, visible for all to see if only they had looked beyond their own concerns. Not deeply, but right there on the surface. The way he reached out and had to purchase love and affection, never having it given to him freely.

There was always a price that had to be paid. For Bobby, I came to realize, the price was always too high. Was it a flaw of his? No, I don't believe so. I believe that it was a wanting that was out of control. To him any warm display of affection directed his way was perceived as love.

He would, in turn become attached to emotions, that surely was naught but bait dangled before him like a worm on a hook used to lure this simple fish in for the kill. Take all that he is worth; they conspired, his money, his offering of support, his food, even though they were not hungry. Take even his emotions and then the person himself, his very soul. Then they would leave him in a state of more wanting than when they had found him. He has been left wounded upon the ground and the sky weeps for him. Nothing can replace the sweetness of his being, nor cleanse the air of his oh so limited existence.

Death begins in the eyes. Its reflection is that of hopelessness. He has spent his life living deep within the lyrics of love songs. The voices and instruments in sweet, slow, perfect harmony, soft and smooth, stimulating him to sway to its mellow tones. Lost he is still, even today. Lost in dreams he dreams of emotions that he had longed to feel, only to awake to the reality that those who raised them from the deep recesses of his being, just toyed with them.

Feelings of love, elation, grief, fear, never joy or happiness, all have brought only pain and agony. In the end all leaving Bobby as he is now, abandoned. Though tired and lacking the desire to go on, he seems to have some form of endurance, some invisible power that is without compromise. It is a force that is driving him always forward to nowhere.

Though where he is, is in reality, no place at all. I have known Bobby all of his life. Now I reflect back through the years to try to determine how he came to be here at this place and time. I assure you, was not a whim on his part. Someone or something lured him here on a promise. He came to where he thought love and a new beginning awaited him. Here in Raleigh North Carolina, on Kemsford Place, he thought he would find comfort at last and dwell therein forever, for always and a day. This time it was not just love that eluded him. This time it was the promise of a simple truth.

What difference is there in his present than what has been in his past? None, nor was there a vision of a difference that he foresaw in his future, if it is at long last death. Maybe death is the beginning of the new him, preserved until the end of time in the form of the written word, pen taken in hand to lay down upon paper the life of a human being.

At last a voice that has gone unheard resounds throughout time into time eternal. His heart poured out onto white pages immortalized in black ink. Time is fraying his soul into torn corners of pages that have been re-read, turned and fingered by hands seeking to feel the full impact of what I have tried to reveal to you. A picture painted with verbs and nouns and adverbs and adjectives, all in vivid colors.

So very unlike his life which was lived only in shades of black and white, colorless and drab. The greens that surrounded him were laced with envy. The reds were just random drops of blood staining a path leading to nowhere. Bright yellow flashed up the backs of men to reveal the cowardice of their inner selves. Then there were the seas of blue that harbored in its depths the hatred that man has for other men. Something inside of him may still remind him of the child he wanted to be. Upon his head you would like to see a halo bright and golden. In reality what you will see is a crown of thorns. Never the less, until his time is through. I know, everyday he will give to others a part of himself that comes from deep within his soul. Here at the end, I hope and pray that these words will make someone out there in this vast expanse we call earth, pay attention to those innocent ones who are dying and who have died for our sins, and maybe per-chance, if you can find the time, cry just a little bit for Bobby.

The Razor and the Mirror

I heard the commotion in the kitchen, the sounds of Herb Oscar Anderson singing his morning song on the radio. The water was running in the kitchen sink where he washed and shaved prior to leaving for work. In our small railroad flat apartment on 129th street, between Madison and Park, there was no sink in the bathroom, just a toilet and a bathtub. Above the bathtub, there was a medicine chest.

On its front was a mirror that was clouded from age, and a ceiling light that, as I remember, worked rarely if ever. So often, I used it to escape into, and to plot my escape from what had, in my short 7 years, become a repetitive style of life. The smell of Old Spice and Noxzema filled the air along with his vocalizing of some modern tune of the day. Even at that early hour, 6:00 a.m., and his joyous mood. I knew that in a few moments, as experience had taught me, he was going to erupt into an intense rage.

My screams of pain and agony would pierce the neighborhood that was always deserted of its residents, except for a few who would walk from mid-block to the corner of 129th street and Madison. This is where, at Mr. Frank's candy store, they could purchase, in a paper cup with a paper lid, a good ten-cent cup of coffee, upon which to sip and savor as they read their New York Daily News and Daily Mirror Newspapers.

They were stacked in neat piles on Mr. Frank's black marble counter. You could also play the numbers if you desired, even brief verbal exchanges were made between Mr. Frank and his customers' as long as the conversation did not become inconvenient so as to distract this skinny, cigar smoking man with a strong South Carolina accent that left one wondering whether or not he was lying about his place of birth and continued residence up until when he arrived in Harlem. His speech led one to believe that Mr. Frank was probably West Indian. The fact of the matter was that he was just a bad talking South Carolina Gullah man.

You became inconvenient, and the conversation unnecessary once you had reached the limit of your purchase power. Once he asked, "What else you need mon?" (His, Mr. Franks, pronunciation of the word man.) If you had no designs on buying anything else, Mr. Frank abruptly said "next," and the kindness and attentiveness that was directed at you, was in an instant shifted from you to the next customer, except on Sundays. Then, along with your newspaper and coffee, you could, for a reasonable cost of 50 cents, purchase yourself a taste of Seagram's Seven or Gordon's Gin, straight up in a Dixie cup. If it was going to be a long Sunday you could also buy a bottle of either, at an inflated price.

Mr. Frank was always at his most expressive display of kindness when selling booze from the back of his candy store. Whenever it seemed that he sold a customer a drink he also poured one for himself. If it is not already apparent to you I will bring the point home more concisely; Mr. Frank liked to taste a bit himself. I always enjoyed him the most once he had tasted himself into joy and lightheartedness.

He became more animated and displayed a sense of humor you not having the pleasure of knowing him would never expect from a man so staunch in his demeanor. I have learned since, a taste or two has a tendency to do that to some people. Other than these routine occurrences, my plight was just beginning to unfold.

As I lay in my bed, the urine sloshing about in a puddle beneath me, the air as usual reeked with the scent of fresh urine. More often than not, I would pile the covers under me in an attempt to soak this foul puddle up into the blanket so that upon inspection, he would find me dry. My attempts always failed. The brown rubber sheet separating me from the mattress held far more than I could conceal. And so every morning I simply waited for the inevitable. When the music stopped and he was clean-shaven, my fate was always sealed. I had known nothing else my entire life.

My very first memory of my father was that of him beating me. Nothing changed that morning, or the next. Being battered and beaten the first thing every morning had become, to me, one of life's many tolerances. For lack of a better explanation, he seemed to hate me with a passion and found great delight in, as he would put it, "tearing that little smart ass, mother-fucker's ass up."

He would say, "The fuck reads all kinds of books and is smarter than his teachers, but he'll lay up in here and piss up my mother-fucking bed," and "I don't like the motherfucker anyway." Those horrible words! "I don't like the motherfucker anyway," always tore through me, burning and searing me to the heart. By seven years old, I had gotten use to the beatings, but the hatred caused me at times to resort to self-mutilation.

That old medicine cabinet mirror often saw the results of my deeply embedded self-hate. I would, in the dim light that was reflected upon it by the redirected sunlight, cast down into the airshaft. There, I in the dimly lit hollow in the rear of a roach-infested railroad flat, take my fathers razor from the medicine cabinet. I would take the blade out and while shifting my face in the mirror, so as to get a more clear view of my self-disdain, set about cutting. Mind you, this was accomplished while balancing myself on the edge of the bathtub that was beneath the medicine cabinet.

And while performing my balancing act, I would take the razor and cut fine lines in my face.

My cheeks, I found to be my favorite mutilation areas. I would take the razor in hand, and in a systematic precise manner proceed to cut small cuts, just so slightly as to cause bleeding. The cuts usually ran from the bridge of my nose toward the ear or down the contour of my cheek toward the chin. With surgical precision I would cut small lines into my face. All in an attempt to, if possible, correct the ugly that was so horrible in its appearance to all, all save a few people, whom I will tell you about later, found me extremely undesirable to look at and were possessed with an overwhelming feeling of discomfort whenever they were in my presence.

So, from as young as 5 years old, I had practiced my surgical techniques. At seven a master at my craft, so masterful that no one ever really noticed-except for a few people, whom, as I have already mentioned, I will tell you about later. People were incapable of remaining still when alone with me. I was often accused of being the cause of one relative or another, not hitting the number, or being the reason why someone's hat was blown from ones head during a gust of warm summer breeze or cast aloft by the suddenness and violence of some north/south cold wind in the winter of the year. No one looked me in my eyes.

They, my relatives, their friends, neighbors

and their children all talked to me with the sides of their faces in my direction. Their eyes darted from left to right as they tried not to make eye contact with me. As if I, a baby of years could in some manner by some demonic gift of grand magnitude granted me from The Bowels of Hades, see into their hearts. That I, by these powers that they thought I possessed, could even if they, in what in all probability was no more than a flickering of an eyelid, after looking into my eyes, that simple act allowed me to see into their hearts.

It was believed that I could see the very soul of a man. Your deepest secrets would be revealed to me in an instant. Of course, I possessed no such power, no insight into what may or may not occur in the future. I could neither on a whimsical thought, flick from the air, what the number was going to be on any given day. Nor could I cause the number to change so as to reap some sort of sweet revenge on any individual who I thought had committed some wrong against me. I was totally incapable of such grand fetes attributed to me.

For reasons that I cannot explain, nor have I given much deliberate pondering upon, why my character, my being and existence brought such discomfort to people. What I did was try to survive as best I could. Most now reside in contrasts of black and gray; they are, from time to time, projected forward from the deep recesses of my memory into my mind's eye. And here briefly they exist once again as substance-less figures. They go in and out of focus as my soul fights to remember their scent, the warmth of life's energy that flowed through them, and the warmth of their breath, Oh, just to see it frost into puffs of smoke as it hits the coldness of an icy sunlit day.

The sound of a voice that is recorded only in my mind as I remember it, what I remember as sounding like a meadowlark in song, may well to someone else sound like the bellowing of a boar hog during mating season. I remember them as I remember them. The one's who, because of their own discomfort around me, would invent infractions of my father's rules that I was supposed to have committed, just to see me whipped and demeaned in environments ranging from Sunday school at my Uncle Paul's church to picnics at Crouton on the Hudson.

They seemed to get some wondrous pleasure watching my dehumanization. As though they were making me pay for having what they thought was a dark and evil gift granted me by the father of all demons from the darkest, deepest bowels of some concept of hell created in those same demented minds that concocted the idea that a child could see into the hearts of men. I cannot now, nor could I then, see any of their lustful thoughts. All the things that they were guilty of were not laid open before me like some heavenly book of Judges.

There was no vision that appeared before

me that revealed their pain or sorrow. I held no mastery over such talents. I was and am a watcher. If any had bothered, they would have realized that it was they that spoke of their hatreds. Their conduct laid bare their hidden lust to me. And I only saw the guilt that they revealed to me. I saw the guilt that they felt after they had accused me of a wrong that I had not committed. It was always after, that they realized how brutal a punishment they had caused to be inflicted on the person of a child. Their degrees of guilt did not always tell me who they were as a person. Their degrees of guilt always revealed to me what type of person they chose to be.

I knew that most did harbor a deep disdain for what they thought that I was. That knowledge only drove me to be more vigilant at and about my work. There grew in me an overwhelming hunger for the bathroom mirror and the razor that relieved me of all the pain. There was always the belief that if I cut away enough or maybe if I cut deep enough, the innocence of my being would be revealed to them, and all would be well. All was not well, nor is it.

So every opportunity that allowed me to gain access to the mirror and the razor I took full advantage of. I would cut ever so gently and precisely, guiding the sharpness of the blade into the skin, always just enough to allow the slightest dribble of blood to emerge from the cut. I would continue relieving my anxieties in this fashion until my cheeks took on the appearance one would expect to see when a woman has gone to the extreme in the application of bright red blush. My cheeks were plump ripe pomegranates with its juices flowing as though its seedlings ruptured and dripped red. The slice and the after-sting is what satisfied my hunger to be free and rid of the blight that I was.

Always feeling like the fruit of ill will, never suitable for harvest, no longer ripe but not yet rotten, fine cuisine for the hogs roaming about this quagmire of an existence, I of so tenderness of years had been thrust into. And he continued to groom. He sang Johnny Ace's last song, "Forever my darling, my love will be true, from now and forever, I'll love only you." His voice was smooth and captivating. I always loved to hear him in those moments right before the savagery that dwelled within him emerged and I became his first and primary object of suppressed rage for the remainder of what turned out to be the entity that I am.

But, anyway he could sing, and I loved the sound of his voice. I also loved Johnny Ace, his voice, existing beyond his earthly capabilities to utter even a simple groan. What he was as a living entity now reduced to the harmonic utterances captured and eternalized on a plastic disk as he was for just those few moments in the time of man. I loved Johnny Ace mainly because he was tragic and he was a worthy person for me to add to my prayers at night.

The more worthy things that I had to pray

for, the longer I stayed awake. The longer I remained awake, the less likelihood of my wetting the bed. If the bed, in all my prayers, I had begged for, was found to be dry. What will it feel like not to have ones first contact with another human being be one of having acts of violence rather than simply seeing the sun rise in the east on a misty morn as a greeting to another day of existence? I often asked myself. I never saw the sunrise neither in the mist nor breaking its way into the sky on a hot muggy beginning of what proved to be a sweltering day.

I lay as motionless as possible, waiting. My head covered. My nostrils singed by the stench of fresh urine, my body covered with bruises and lacerations from previous beatings, bed wettings, or other violations of minor or created "infractions" of his or any other rule he, at that second, decided to enforce. The lacerations burned as I lay in wait of the inevitable. I suppose that one of two things occurred, one being: I could not come up with enough people who I deemed worthy enough to pray for, or that would permit me to indulge in fervent prayer throughout the course of the night, or two, being: I was simply a little boy who, even though frightened witless, just fell asleep because he was tired?

Yeah, Johnny Ace had blown his brains out while involved in a game of Russian roulette. He had everything to live for and threw it all away in one foolish moment.

And here I, a lowly thing who had naught to

look forward to but the same from day to day, found great delight in this sensation that we experience and refer to as life. I was fascinated by what each new experience I would encounter when next I'd ask a stranger, "Where are you from?" For me to be deprived of such a grand adventure would be a travesty.

The thought of being in a condition of non-existence, death, revolted me. I always refrained from touching lovingly, or kissing with affection some dead relative. In my youthful wisdom I had already determined that for one to dress up a piece of meat stiff and cold from lacking the internal spark that warms us with animation—to put this piece of meat on display before it starts to rot and repulse others with its stench, in an expensive carton. Just so that people will say, "The undertaker sho did a good job." "Looked like him or her self." Or, "So and so was sho put away nice." Well, to me, and all that I was concerned with was how I viewed this practice.

To me the dead do not look like they are asleep or at rest. And as a matter of fact, no man or woman dresses in their Going-To-Church-Clothes, and lies down for prolonged slumber unless drink, drugs or sudden illness causes that repose. No. I never uttered the words, "Him or her sure looks natural." He or she looked dead, dead is not natural. I avoided them. I did not feel comfortable engulfed in the chill that is emitted from them. That chill, that seems to linger only in their proximity.

I too greatly enjoyed life's warmth. Now, on the other hand, I found great pleasure in walking among them once they were entombed. I found great pleasure in the sharing of their peace and solitude. Often I thought that men should envy them there in the place of the tombs. Stranger dwells next to stranger and neither tries to exert greater power over the other. Never a hateful word exchanged between them. No longer are they men and women of race, creed or nation. They are no longer black, white, red or yellow. They are now, all just dead. They are, all just dead. Death, it seemed in this grand scheme of things, is the only pure form of equality known to mankind. Dead is just dead. What difference does it make to the dead who else is dead the better or who has been dead the longest? Dead is just dead.

He continued to go about his morning routine of grooming himself. Elegant, flawless and composed was what he projected to the entire world. I knew all of his flaws and weaknesses. It was I who knew his pain and agony better than he himself. Delighted was I whenever I saw him move with panther-like grace in, through and about those with whom he found pleasure in their company. I, alone, felt and endured his real inner-self.

That person, who, on that morning like all the rest, would attack me with the pervasiveness of a strong well-manned lion protecting his territory, so I waited for what would without a doubt take place. Soon the covers would be jerked off me with the suddenness of a crack of thunder on a clear day, and my day would begin. This morning, though, I had made a decision that would prove to be one of the poorest and yet most crucial of my young life.

On this morning I decided not to run from my punishment. No matter how painful. This morning there would be no more mournful pleas for mercy and surely this morning and never again would I cry. My heart rate elevated as it always did in anticipation of his abrupt attack on my person. Lying there with my arms crossed over my chest, I felt the pounding of my heart. The rapidity and intensity was almost maddening. The sensation was such that it made me believe at times that my small heart was going to explode.

The pounding swishing sound only helped to intensify my fear. Softly I would inhale and exhale. If I made no sound maybe this time he will pass me by and this awakening this morn, would tenderly embrace me in its new beginning. This, I thought, as my small undeveloped muscles would tense, then quiver, then relax, and tense only to quiver again in contemplation over what part of my body would be struck first and with what. I, knowing from experience that all of my body parts, would in its own turn, receive its own attention, maybe this time, a punch to the back of the head.

Maybe the slant of wood that prevented me from rolling out of the bed and onto the floor. The belt always followed, never the first or the only instrument used to rid me of my desire, as he would put it, to piss his bed just because, as he thought, I just out of spite wanted to. The morning beating was a means of relieving me of such desires.

This morning it was the fist to the back of the head first. The impact drove my face into the wall with such force that plaster from the wall, and paint chips fell to the floor in clumps spattering on the floor. The fact that my head was wrapped in the covers may very well that morning, without a doubt afforded me an escape from serious injury. The impact none-the-less made me flail through what was now a kaleidoscope world.

Stunned, colors moving in wave's brilliant, but strongly out of focus, ducking and dodging in an attempt to avoid the next blow. Blinded by the force of his blow, I had nowhere to run, blinded; I could not seek a place in which to hide myself. At his mercy, but not as what was the norm. This time there were no pleas. There was no outcry. As was the norm I did not jump immediately from the bed crying mournfully that I would never pee the bed again. Did I beg for clemency as was usual? No, "No more please don't hurt me." No! This was going to be the morning that I would begin the day that I would get satisfaction.

That morning I was determined that he was not, ever again, going to demean and brutalize me and walk away feeling as though he had accomplished his mission to break my spirit. That morning it was determined that there would be no tears, no submission. From this day forward my inner self was screaming "You will have to kill me before I ever again suffer openly at your hands." Though, at the same instant, I was thinking, "Will it hurt when I die?"

He began to slap and punch at my covered head. "Get up you filthy, nasty son of a bitch," he screamed, as the slapping and punching continued. When I tried to comply, I was struck in the face and my mouth filled with blood and its copper-sweet taste was overpowering. With one hand he dragged me from the top bunk bed slamming me hard on to the floor. With the other, he drew his belt from its loops. This day, it was a silver-black narrow plastic one. The edges always left cuts in my flesh, leaving the outline of its shape imprinted deeply in my flesh.

Raising me in the air by one of my arms, he lashed me over and over about my back, arms, and buttocks, wherever it landed skin was broken and bruises appeared. I jerked and twitched but did not flail about, nor did I cry. This response to his beating, on my part, seemed to enrage him even more. "You're not going to cry." "Huh!" "Mother-Fucker!" "You're not going to cry?" Huh?"

My underclothing was saturated with fresh urine. And each time that he struck me, urine would spray off of me wherever the belt made contact. He huffed and puffed with each blow as though he was trying with all of this might to slice me in half.

Inside there was that desire to try to break free to avoid the blows as I fought not to yell out for mercy. But, I did neither. He beat and beat and beat me. When, because his hands were sweating, the belt would escape his grasp. He would kick at me and knee me as he searched about the floor for his instrument of punishment. At some point in time during the beating he somehow managed to strike me with the buckle of the belt. Most of the blows landed about my face and head. One blow ripped into my penis, tearing the foreskin. I have never been circumcised, so the foreskin being ripped caused blood to flow down my leg. The pain made me pray for unconsciousness. "You little cock sucker." "You had better *not* get any blood on my clothes," he yelled.

While he caught his breath, I crawled into the living room, following me every time I was able to crawl a few feet away from him, he would kick me over onto my side and use the belt. Once even pinning me to the floor on my back he stood astride me punching and slapping me. Exhausted, he fell back onto the living room chair. "I'm going to kill your fucking ass." "This fucking morning, you little prick." Puffing hard he said, "I'm going to kick your ass until you cry." "You think that you're more man than I am?" Kicking me as I lie curled in a ball at his feet. My little body would convulse and he would kick or strike me again. "Get the fuck up and put your clothes on over top that pissed up shit," he said, still out of breath, and hang that sheet out the front window so everybody can see that your smart ass still pisses the bed."

"The next time I kick your ass you'll cry motherfucker, or I'll kill you." He said, as I crawled out of his striking range. He sat with his legs stretched out in front of himself, exhausted. Pop was six feet two inches tall, slender, but well defined muscularly. His teeth were white and aligned perfectly, except for the two front upper teeth. They were lost when knocked out when he had fallen from the back of a streetcar while hitching a ride on the back of it. His hands! His hands! Oh! How smooth and flawless. They were as soft as a gentle westward sea breeze lying gently on the coast of Maine in the twilight of the day.

To say that he was simply handsome would be a raging understatement. Those large brown eyes captivated me because in them, if you looked deep enough, could see what his heart wanted to reveal. They told you, if you listened intensely, that there was a deep-seated pain. They told you of a sadness that made him so, so very weak and empty.

So hollow and empty this feeling of sadness I saw though his eyes. Then there were times, I always stared at people, when, if I had not exerted great will power, gazing into them brought me to the brink of deep vocal sobbing and emotional despair.

The almond tone of his skin only enhanced these deep brown beautifully shaped orbs. The flawless almond tone was beautiful, and as flawless as a perfect pearl. Partly due to the ethnic properties of this once human being, very little hair grew on his face. His hair was black and looked like smooth brushed oiled satin. Even at 6:00 in the evening, he looked and smelled as though he had only moments before stepped from the barber's chair. Pop was himself American Indian. A combination of three different ethnic groups in reality: From the tribes of the Kusso Natchez and Cherokee, mixed with French and Portuguese.

I have already mentioned how his every move was panther-like. Even when moving quickly, he was a picture of grace, he always seemed to just flow like velvet through whatever environment he was in. I, supposing, considering what you have just read, are wondering, "Where are the horns and pointed-tail?" Contrary to what opinion one has formed, I didn't see The Devil when I sometimes for hours would stare at him. When caught, I paid dearly. He hated when I stared, especially at him.

My father was generous to a fault. He would feed you if you were hungry put a few dollars in your pocket if you were broke. There were times when he would permit a family member or friend to spend a few nights in our home. He couldn't bear to see a person without a roof over his or her head. I loved walking in pubic with him. Everybody knew and respected him. "Hey, Dick, what's a good number for today?" One would yell as we would walk pass a cleaners. "My man Dick," another would say just in passing. "Dickerson, missed you Friday," a woman would say while running her hand against his. "I have my boys with me," he would respond referring to my older brother Delroy and me. "I'll be at the Lucky Spot later sweetheart," he would say with a wink. "Check with me later." The woman would prance off in glee, with the anticipation of what the night might bring.

Those big brown eyes would captivate women and he could disrobe them with a glance or a wink. He served them up what they wanted most, himself, and they rewarded him with clothes, cologne (the finest), and money that he would use to gamble with. Pop loved to play cards, as did all of the men in his family, he would use the money to pay bills or to buy food and special gifts for my mother, my brother Delroy or my sisters. It was rare indeed when I would reap the same benefits of his ill-gotten gains, as did my siblings.

As was the norm, I was restricted or should I say relegated (always after the beating) to punishment or punishment related duties, such as being restricted to my bed, only being permitted to leave it if nature were to beckon. Or I would be made to sit with my back facing the television, surely as a means of depriving me of visual entertainment.

Delroy would "Ooh!" and "Wow!" in an attempt to get me to turn around. That simple response reflex always brought more wrath and restrictions. Delroy always seemed to find great delight in stirring up conflict between Pop and I. It was rare when Delroy was punished, if spanked, Mom and Pop would cry afterwards and with great tender affection, comfort him. From my first memory of Delroy, it was apparent that he had mastered putting on the guise of innocence.

"You make me just want to kill you!" These were about as tender the words as I could expect. Looking beyond them, as far as I was concerned, constituted foolish hope. Staring had made me wise beyond my years. I had learned, by watching that it would be unwise to put myself in a position that would lead others to believe me to be a fool. And that I would be that much more lacking in wisdom, if I were to put my hopes in a fool. Foolish it would have been if I were to expect anything more than what I had received. I learned to expect the expected.

The void, what was lacking in my life, was simple acts of love. My! How I would have found total contentment in a warm embrace or a kind word. I was not the recipient of either. I, for the purpose of survival, just took things as they came. The family often said that I had a way about me. Whatever that way was, they despised.

Delroy was the cute, innocent one. Everybody loved and lavished gifts on him. As for me, they just uncomfortably tolerated my presence. It is also important that you understand that I always took advantage of their discomfort. If I entered the front door, the room became quiet. Whatever had been taking place prior to my arrival stopped instantly. They said I had a way about me from birth. I was different much, much more so than the other children. I was old and tired, worn and battered. Playing with children was something that I did because it was expected of me. Not because I enjoyed playing with them, they were, as a matter of fact, a bore to me. They were not what I considered competition on any level. They played. I learned and I absorbed. I had nothing in common with them or the games that they played.

My family and others must have sensed this oddity about me. Even now in the evening of my days, I often wonder what is it that I am that God has created. If one were to compare me to what is the norm concerning human behavior, most surely I would be considered an oddity. Unlike those considered the norm, I pondered on why they, the norm, lacked any natural affection for one another.

Watching them, I deduced that most, would, without any feelings of guilt, steal, lie and cheat to get what was a benefit to them. Not, mind you what was a necessity in their lives in order to subsist. Most just wanted what they wanted. If it were your husband or wife they would try to seduce him or her just to satisfy some filthy desire. Pop just wanted what he wanted just like all the rest of those selfish people that I despised. The women that I encountered traveling about the city and bars with him just seemed to want Pop.

It was a common occurrence when we would be out with Pop. Often we would end up sitting in front of the television in some strange woman's apartment, while he and the woman spent time together in her bedroom. Delroy's distraction was easily bought with hotdogs, ice cream and candy. I, on the other hand, always took great offense. The mere fact that he was with a woman other than my mother gave me no appetite, nor was I distracted into complacency by treats while listening to and having to endure the grunts, groans and screeches of passion emitting from the bedroom of some woman that was not my mother. I, to this day, can still remember the hot, pungent, offensive smell of sex on him. I remember the odor as one that was an offense to my underdeveloped senses.

Wonder, I still, as to why my mother did not vomit every time he touched her upon returning home. If I, at so tender an age, could recognize odors that were surely caused by the after effects of a sexual encounter, most surely she must have, and rather than fight she just chose to endure. My mother, today, as I write, has mastered enduring. There were many days of her life filled with despair and anger. The despair she tolerated, her anger most often than not was taken out on me.

Mom would cuddle Delroy, Edith, Katie and Theresa. I was the object of her venting. At times, the brutality was equal to that of my father. Whatever was near at hand became an instrument used to inflict punishment. Once she even beat me about the head with a military steel helmet. I had informed her that she was mistaken concerning a matter. The beating was because she said that I had called her a liar. My mother's treatment of me both confused and hurt me.

When my dad failed to return home from work on a Friday night and we were left with no food for dinner, I would go out into the evening, and from block to block and trashcan to trashcan, look for soda bottles. These bottles rendered a deposit for their return. Some were worth two cents; the 32 oz bottles were worth five cents. When I had obtained enough to purchase food, I would return home with enough food for the weekend and ice Pops or ice cream cones for my siblings. It was rare that I would benefit from my efforts. Usually, I was punished for staying out after the streetlights came on.

Often sent to bed without dinner while the others, who had contributed nothing, would savor the delights I had unselfishly worked for and provided for the household. Upon his return from whomever he had been with or, wherever he had been, Pop would bring Mom deli treats: corned beef on rye, Carvel milk shakes or a bottle of perfume. The perfume, she never wore because our apartment was her prison. She rarely left the house. Her children were her jail keepers. While she ate in contentment, I could hear her giving pop a report on my conduct. "So you think you're a mother-fucking man, do you?" He would yell in anger en-route to wherever I was hiding. I would brace myself for the expected. "I fucked for you cocksucker, you didn't fuck for me."

As the physical abuse began, my Mom would continue to eat and sip as though nothing was taking place. Other than the occasional stirring and shaking of her milk shake to loosen the ice cream in her shake so that it would flow smoothly through the straw, or to readjust the over abundance of meat, which is indicative of a New York deli sandwich, as it squeezed out of her sandwich and sometimes wiping the juice from her chin, juice that seeped from the succulent kosher pickle that served as a flavor enhancement to her corned beef on rye. She never paid any attention to the abuse of her child, me. I, rather than receiving affection, was relegated to suffer her total disinterest and endure his rage and brutality.

What strange feelings surged thunderously through my young mind when the pain of rejection was a prevailing factor in my fragile short time upon the surface of this planet Earth. Often I would wonder what a warm and loving embrace would feel like. To be touched gently and held tightly next to a pounding heart against someone's breast, to smell the sweet fragrant odor of pure affection, rather than the stench of ever emitted hate and loathing.

Wonder, did I, so very often, what it would feel like to exist, but for one day without pain so undeserved, to hear my name spoken in tender tones like the song of a nightingale, soothingly called upon to share in the joys of normal humans. I would have loved to have been able to provoke laughter, rather than scorn.

What manner of beast is it that I am that the great God of men has created? What could be so vile that upon seeing me, scourging the beast is the only thought that enters the minds of all else human? What pleasure do they find within themselves by causing me so much injury? What unwanted gift had God given me that proved to be a curse that compels others to become vile in an unnatural manner toward me?

What about this gift that repels rather than, attracts, this gift that provokes other to rip my heart from my small and affectionate breast, a tiny heart that with every beat longs to be accepted and throbs with a pure and majestic desire just to please, a warm heart filled with loneliness and wanting. A wanting only understood by the innocence of a child's mind.

Wonder, did I, and do I still, why the heart must remain broken and pained. Never knowing a comforting word directed his way, never embraced by love nor overflowed with glee, eyes that have never seen except through tears. My world was distorted and abstract. Bent like a pencil viewed through a water filled glass, a tongue that should be savoring the sweetness of youth, tastes only the bitter saltiness of constantly flowing tears of rejection. As I have already stated, "What manner of beast be I?"

I am son to no mother or father, brother without sister or brother, friend to none, without hope, loved by no one. Alone in a world occupied by millions, noticed by none, naught but by my own shadow, and it too rejects me when befriended by the shadows cast by others, or embraced by the light of day or caressed by a moonless night.

My only companion was the mirror and the razor. It was at this early age that I came to realize that without a doubt pains and agonies do indeed make strange bedfellows. The mirror, the razor and I were a family of three. Two comforting, enabling inanimate objects and one tormented soul, worthless, vile and deserted by humans but released from agony and the searing pains of life in their cold embrace. After all, there was no charge for the pleasure found when I was with them, nor was there contempt.

One just allowed me to view within its defects, my own. The other, a slicing means by which to correct the contempt others held for me. To remove it, however, proved to be much more of a task than I could perform, I, never being able to cut deep enough to remove enough, never enough to satisfy their desire to rid them of me. It was the comfort that I got out of my attempt to rid myself of the beast that I was. Once in a while the sight of the pulsating vein in my neck would compel me to try to slice deeply into it.

Halted, was I, by the thought of being beaten and abused by my father as the life's blood shot in streams and spurts from my dying body. Not because I had inflected a mortal wound upon myself, but because I would have made a mess in his bathroom. So strange was my reasoning, fearing him more than death. Suppose, did I that it was better to live than to be subjected to another beating when death would have been the ultimate escape from my life in hell. Though now I believe that it would have been better for me if decomposed into grave tar I had become, than to have lived so long as I have. Cast aside and rejected by people who should have loved me.

Beneath a covering of earth I would now lay in a dreamless sleep, maggots would have become my soft bedding and worms spread over me as a comforting covering. Youthful, I would have gone back to the earth. The maggots, finding equal delight in the eating of my flesh as they would one who men had placed in the ground at eighty. Therein, they, the maggots and the worms, find no difference. Nor is the meat of a child any sweeter there in the darkness and silence than that of a man of eighty. Meat is simply meat to them.

The flesh of a child differing not from the flesh of a person who died of old age, in the end, what they do not eat turns to dust. Even now, oh! Even now, there is a longing deep down in the bowels of my being for the silence of the grave, a longing to hear the roar of joy on the other side of the silence. For in this lifetime I have dressed in the finest of garb. I have fought against men in mortal combat. Cut the throats of generals and holy men. Ridden upon the backs of the swiftest of ponies, and danced until dawn with the most comely of harlots. Drunk I have been on the best of wines, but still I am despised and ridiculed for being different.

I have planted seeds of life, and not partaken of its harvest, drank from the goblet filled with success and thirst I do still to succeed. Knowledgeable it is that I am. Yet I have learned nothing. Sleep has found me, but it is rest that has eluded me. Love for a woman, I have longed for, sought and given. The recipient of love I have not been. All these things have been told to you so that I can tell you more, more about the beginning? You would think. No. Not even about the end. There has never been a beginning because it has always been. And, in the end you decide if it has really ended at all, or is the end my beginning?

But, now if you will permit me, let me take you back to where I left off. He, my father, upon his return from whoring or gambling would without fail, always bring savory delights for all, but me. Always short one hero sandwich, one ice cream cone, and one corned beef on rye. He would force me to sit with my brother and sisters as they enjoyed partaking of his guilt offering. They would snicker and tease as they licked and chewed and smacked. "Bobby's begging daddy," they in turn would yell. He would enter the room and inflict some form of injury on my person, an open-handed smack to the head. Being thrown to the floor and kicked or have his foot placed firmly on my neck was not uncommon. What was common was my going to bed hungry.

He would rant and rave over the fact that I had supported his wife and children during his absence, "Fuck you!" "You work!" "Buy your own food." He would yell at me. Hunger was a constant in my life whenever I tried to do what was right. I was punished and starved for doing what I thought was the right thing. Another job that I worked during his jaunts and rivals was for Berney the butcher. His shop was on Madison Avenue between 129th and 128th streets between Dr. Mill's drug store and Mr. & Mrs. Taylor's grocery store.

In those days of my childhood, the grocery and fish merchants would sweep out and put down new saw dust at closing. Mr. Berney paid me 10 cents to perform that duty. It was also part of my responsibility to wash and stone down the butcher blocks. Ten cents would buy a stick of butter or a small loaf of Silver cup bread. A dime went a long way for a family of 6 when a dime was all that you had. A loaf of bread and some canned government meat made an excellent sandwich when hunger pangs would be your company throughout the night. Bread and butter sandwiches took the edge off. And was as welcomed as steak and potatoes, if that was all you had to eat.

More times than not, as the supplier, I still would go without. My punishment for staying out after the street light had come on. If I had not, there would have been nothing to eat at all for the others. So, some nights when restricted to my bed, I would, from the shattered plaster in the wall, gouge myself on small chunks of it just to have the flavor of something in my mouth. Happy that my mother was eating even if it was food consumed through tears.

There in Berney's Butcher shop was a fat black man with one eye larger than the other. He operated the vegetable stand part of the store. So fat was he that the only time that he stood was to weigh the vegetables that he sold to the local residents of the area. All other times he could be found seated on a tall stool. I developed a great fear of him early on in our association. He always wanted to touch me, no matter when he saw me he would offer me a nickel or a dime. The eye that was larger than the other pierced my very soul. Something vile and wicked dwelled deep within it. The way it focused on me caused me great discomfort and unexplained fear.

Had I not been innocent, maybe I would have been able to avoid what happened to me on October 11th, the eve of my eighth birthday. Mr. Berney had paid me my ten cents and left before the fat man with the large eye. I was sweeping behind the counter when I sensed someone behind me. There he was naked from the waist down smiling. The eye seemed larger than I had ever seen it before and he was pulling hard in a back and forth motion on his penis. Fear thrust me into silence as he came toward me. He said, "Just relax." "Let me just rub this against your pretty little ass." I couldn't utter a sound for what seemed like an eternity. When I could, all I was able to say was, "Please!" There was nowhere to run.

One of the large butcher blocks was situated right in front of where I could exit from behind the counter. The attempt that I made was futile in its exercise and I was thrown face down across the butcher block still wet with bone, meat and blood. Even today, I can still feel and smell its foulness. He pulled down my pants and grunted as he ripped into my anus, pounding and thrusting. I could hear myself being ripped apart and feel the warm blood as it poured down my leg. I tried to scream, but couldn't. The sounds that I wanted to emit got caught mid-throat and only a hiss would emerge. The pain was blinding.

What seemed like hours in reality only lasted a few minutes. When he ejaculated in me it burned so bad that I thought he had inserted fire into me. He expelled a long, high-pitched cry of relief and stood back. Sliding to the floor, the only thing I could say was, "Why?" He replied, "Because you make my dick hard." Then he walked over to his stool and took a nickel from it and threw it at me. "If you tell anybody, they won't believe you." He said. I pulled up my pants, picked up the nickel and never went back to Berney's Meat Market again. Until now, I have never told anybody this story.

With the nickel, I walked over to Mr. and Mrs. Taylor's Grocery store and bought a pound of white potatoes. I bled for weeks, often concealing my shame and the bleeding by rolling old newspaper and placing it between my legs. That night they ate government corned beef and potatoes for dinner, and everyone got two slices of bread. My mother smacked me and sent me to bed. The streetlights had come on before I got home.

I cried myself into a deep, but restless sleep. The pain had alleviated me of any hunger pangs I could have felt. I couldn't even take a bath because the landlord, Leo, had not brought any coal for the boiler and there was no hot water. I did, however eat some plaster from the hole in the wall beside my bed. The morning would bring its own problems anew, I thought as I buried the damp blanket under me to act as a buffer between the still wet sheets and my ravaged body. Maybe this time, I pondered, the blankets will absorb it all and relief from pain will be a welcomed stranger the morning next.

Once again, expectations unfulfilled, I was soaked, raw and burning. My anus throbbed and the blood had turned into a hard crust that sliced and stabbed as I tensed and relaxed from the onset and passing of tension that was building inside of me. The desire to touch the area was overcome by the shame that I felt. Shame concerning what had happened to me the evening last. Was I going to turn into a homosexual? Was there now some deep seeded pleasure that was going to manifest itself in me at a later age? Will he once again seek me out and find me alone and rape me at his will? My mind turned and churned in a pool of confusion and bewilderment.

Giving no thought at all to the plight or the rage that I was, as always, about to face. The newspaper had dried into the blood and I was wondering how to go about removing it without causing an excessive amount of bleeding. Another concern was infection. There were already far too many of those on my person. Specifically, on my thighs and hips caused by the injuries Pop had inflicted on me during his beatings and my being forced to lie in pools of my own urine caused them to fester. The foreskin near the head of my penis was also infected. Most of them I had picked away at or squeezed the pus out of. Now, this, I feared, I would have to contend with also.

The underpants had long ago dry-rotted and turned golden in color from exposure to urine and constant wear. A rusted safety pin held them together between my legs. Sometimes while out and about, the safety pin would detach itself and embed itself into my scrotum. Now, there is a pain that I cannot describe by putting pen to paper to form the words, but I learned to hide it long enough to seek out a private place to which to go in order to correct the problem. I would readjust the situation and go along my life's path, no matter how rocky. It had just simply become a way of life for me.

Sometimes it happened, sometimes it didn't. This way of life was not a matter of choice for me, you must understand, it was a matter of fact. Delroy on the other hand slept with a pillow upon clean white sheets, I rolled up my coat and used it for a pillow. His PJ's were Davy Crockett, Captain Video and Howdy Doody. His under clothes were always clean and fresh every day. Mom would comb and brush his hair in the morning making sure his hand's, arms, legs, and face had ample portions of sweet smelling Jergens lotion rubbed lovingly into every pore.

Always careful making sure that the part in his hair was straight. There was never a hair out of place.

She and Pop made sure that he never left home without getting a loving kiss on the cheek and a pat on the head. I never left home without receiving a good swift kick in the ass and an "I wish you would go to hell." Little did they realize that in my young fragile mind I felt as though it was hell that I was leaving, and that kick in the ass was the jump-start that I needed every morning to help me cope with the rest of life's ups and downs that were lurking outside of Hell's gates, dwelling in Hell's backyard's.

Flowering in the soil fertilized with the manure of human hate and misunderstanding, a garden of evil and strife that I find myself tripping and stumbling through daily. I was pricked and punctured by its thorns, denied the sweet taste of its fruits, finding no comfort beneath the shade of its trees, no peace in the melody of its Robin's song. Rather. I am chased by its Hell's hounds, in the guise of men. What should be an engulfing of angelic light is, in fact, searing heat emitted by a demonic hell fire that burns my tender being to a cinder.

When I thirst for cool flowing waters of love, I am dowsed with boiling lava embedded with stones of hate. Even today, I thirst still. Even today bares little difference from my yesterdays. Nor will my tomorrows be any different. I see little to be gained tomorrow.

But for now let us go back to yesterday, the morning of October 13th 1957. I had just turned eight years old, the day before; I had been raped, punished for doing the right thing again and now lay in wet burning violated silence waiting to be beaten. But, he wasn't home. A reprieve? No, again dashed hopes. I heard the front door unlock and he entered singing happy birthday "Happy birthday to you, happy birthday to you, happy birthday Edie and Theresa, happy Birthday to you.

He had gone to Brooks Bakery on 125th street, a wonderful Jewish bakery located right off of Park Avenue. The best baked goods in Harlem. He always ordered the birthday cakes from there. They were beautiful with white butter cream icing and pineapple filling. He would buy one for Delroy and Katie, Delroy's Birthday was August 12th, and Katie's was August 15th. Edie's was September 15th, and Theresa's was October 1st. As I have already told you, rare was I ever included. But this morning's beating was not going to destroy the positive mood he had planned for the others that day.

He walked up to the side of my bed and grabbed me around the neck in a chokehold and growled, "Don't get your nasty fucking ass out of this bed today." Then he smiled at the girls and reached into the shopping bag that he was carrying and gave each of them a party hat and party favors. To Delroy he gave a golden cardboard crown, saying, "How's daddy's little man today?" I turned my face toward the wall and buried it in my folded coat and cried silently as the others teased me calling me "Pee bed bally butt."

Pop walked into the kitchen and I could hear him singing and rattle about under the sink for the pots and pans as he prepared to cook breakfast. I smelled the pork chops being fried along with sage sausages and home fried potatoes and fried apples. There were fresh parker house rolls and brown onion gravy and everyone was laughing and playing.

Pop was telling Mom that relatives were coming over and that aunt so and so was bringing a ham and cousin what's her name was making Hop "n" John and Red Rice and turkey and uncle you know who and his wife were bringing a fifth of this and that and a plate of some of this and some of that. Mom was as giddy as a schoolgirl on her first date as she pressed the ribbons for the girl's hair and picked out the best dresses for them to wear.

I lay in my own waste as they ate and planned their day. It was a though I didn't even exist. Nobody even bothered to ask, "Is Bobby going to eat?" Mom never knew that the potatoes and bread that she had eaten the night before came at a price that I should not have had to pay, my innocence. I only hope it was as filling as the meal she and her children were eating now. The flavor seemed to be far more appealing than that which I had provided. "Daddy, Bobby's crying," Edie said. I heard Pop stomp to the side of the bed, "You crying motherfucker?" "No!" I said. "What the fuck you mean no!" "Bitch!" he said. And he punched me in the back so hard that my heart seemed to have stopped beating. "No sir!" I shouted back "No sir!" "Your nasty ass better not be crying." "Get the fuck up and wash those dishes." "Now, you little cock sucker!" He roared.

As I got up the urine dripped from me and on to the floor all the way to the kitchen. There wasn't any food left except for some home fries stuck to the bottom of the black cast iron frying pan. Pop had put water in it to help loosen them from the pan and there was one Parker House roll left. I washed the plates, knives, forks, and spoons and glasses first, saving the cast iron frying pan for last.

When he was out of the kitchen, and no one was looking I poured the water from the pan and scraped the remnants of the home fries out with a spoon and ate them quickly. They were cold greasy and soggy, but I was very hungry, but I was not willing to risk eating the roll, it's absence would be easily discovered and the price to pay would have proved to have been much too high.

So content I was with what I had been able to scavenge. At and about my duties I went until completion. Then I crawled back into the wetness of my confinement, and the stench of my existence. To linger in the burning agony of my being, praying to a God that seemed to have forgotten that it was he who was responsible for my being created. What if he too had taken offense in his own creation? What if even he too was capable of making a mistake that could not be corrected. Or was this my punishment for having once serving God in heaven as a powerful angel and not being content to serve him as he created me, inside longing in my heart for the desires of mortal man? What if?

The misguided and bewildered malformed thoughts of a child were what held me up through the weary days and comforted me during the nights. After all, I was just brilliant, not wise. Pop had opened the windows and it was rather cool in the room lying there in that pool of urine. Bundled as best as I could against the chill wind that blew in through the windows from down the garbage filled airshaft that separated my building number 60 from its sister adjoining building number 62. Pop said it was to air out his fucking house for company, who for the sake of continued conversation, was just beginning to arrive even as Mom was dressing the girls in her and Pop's bedroom.

The first to arrive was Pop's first cousin, his name was Goldie Reed a handsome but loud man with a quick temper and very prone to using a knife to cool it whenever it flared up. "Cuz where the tastes?" He said as he came through the door. "Where you left them mother fucker, that's where," Pop replied. They laughed and hugged and joked some more. Cousin Goldie asked, "Where are the birthday children?" "Getting dressed," Pop replied, "Here!" "This is for them, something for their pocketbooks." "Is that other motherfucker here?" Cousin Goldie asked. "He's here," Pop said, "In bed pissed up." "I almost killed that punk again this morning." "He's going to be the cause of me doing something." "I just know it," Pop said in an angry detached tone. Cousin Goldie responded, "You need to put his ass away somewhere before you do." "If he where mine I'd have fucked him up a long time ago." "I'd cut his shroat."

For some reason Cousin Goldie had a great deal of trouble pronouncing the words throat, three and throw correctly. "I'd cut his shroat while he was asleep and carry his dead ass out to Far Rockaway and shrow him in the ocean." "Fuck it Dick," "I'll cut the cock sucker's shroat for you right now." "Roll him in that fucking blanket, and get rid of his ass once and for all." He was yelling as he walked at a fast pace toward my bed. Pop was yelling. "Not now Goldie the other children are here, not now Goldie!" Cousin Goldie by this time was at the peak of his anger and had pulled my head from beneath the covers and yanked my head backwards by my hair. I didn't say a word though. I just stared at him. "What you looking at you evil little fuck?" "What you looking at?" "I'll tell you," "the last fucking thing you ever going to see cock-sucker!"

Pop was reaching for his hand but wasn't

fast enough to stop him from getting to his knife. I heard it snap open and felt the coldness of the blade pressed against my neck. Mom yelled, "Goldie!" "Goldie!" "Why you want to mess up my good sheets?" "Why you want to mess up my good sheets?" "Is Florence coming Goldie?" She asked as she inched her way up to him placing her hand over the hand that was holding the knife against my throat and slowly pulling back she removed it. "Is Florence coming Goldie?" She asked again smiling. "She's coming Annie." He said puffing heavily, "she coming with Brook and Jessie and the kids." "Sit down Goldie and I'll bring you a drink." "Come on." And she put her arm around his shoulder and walked away from me and back into the living room.

On the way to the kitchen she smacked me in my face and said in a whisper, "Do you see what you make people do?" "Damn Goldie, you were really going to kill that son of a bitch weren't you?" Pop laughingly said. "As sure as shit is brown and stinks, I was, Dick." "Ha!" "Ha!" "Somebody needs to." "Did you see the way he just laid there looking at me?" "Real empty like." "There's nothing inside of him Dick!" "Nothing," "Nothing at all except that smart ass shit." "All that smart ass shit is all that he knows." "He doesn't know anything else." "Always making grown folks look stupid." "You know what I mean?" "I know what you mean Goldie." Pop responded.

"But he lies up in that bed every fucking night and will piss and piss to his hearts content." "I mean I'll fuck him up." "Like I would fuck up a man, and it does no good." Cousin Goldie interrupts, "He's just wicked and evil and he controls all of us." "He's got to go or die, Dick." "It has to be one or the other." "He's fucking up this family." "We close man," "we close, all of us, always been close, except for him." "He just makes all of the family uncomfortable just being around him." "You should have kicked him out of Annie's belly before he was born." Pop asked, "You all feel that way?" "Hell yes, all except Book and Jessie." "They want to take him if you and Annie will give him up." "I'll see him dead first," Pop said. "I'll see him dead first."

"Then let's get him dead Dick." "It'll be cheaper then feeding him." Pop said, "I don't half feed the bastard anyway." "He just won't die." And they both broke into this gut generated sinister kind of laughter.

At eight years and one day I lay listening to my father plot my murder with his first cousin, and all I could think about was how wonderful it would be if I could find a few stolen moments in this day to share with the mirror and the razor.

My thoughts were distracted by the knock at the door, "Calabochi, my main man!" That's what Pop called his other first cousin, Charles Reed. He called him that because he was so cool and thought he was cute, but he too was dangerous and would cut you to ribbons with his black mother of pearl handled straight razor while still smiling. All the men in Pop's family were dangerous.

"Cal-la-boo-chi!" Pop said, in a loud voice. "What's up?" Cousin Charles said, "Dick, you know," "The sky, the Sun, the moon, the stars, and me!" "As always clean as a broke dick dog fucking his way through a pound full of hot bitches." "You couldn't fuck your hand motherfucker!" Cousin Goldie said laughing loudly. "I fucked Florence." Cousin Charles said reaching into his inside coat pocket where he always carried his razor. Goldie snapped open his knife, and replied, "Then bitch you must have the clap, cause I gave it to her last night." They laughed and hugged each other and sat down and poured each other a drink. Sipping on his drink cousin Charles asked Pop, "Where's Bobby?" "I brought this gift for him." "I know how much he wanted this book so I had Connie pick it up for him." "It's all the shit written by a cat named Edward Albert Paul, I think." "Connie picked it up for me downtown."

Wow, I thought to myself as I sat straight up in my bed. What he meant to say was the complete works of Edgar Allen Poe, my idol. Miss Connie was Cousin Charles wife she was cool too, and she always treated me well. Pop said, "His ass is on punishment," "I'll give it to him." Cousin Charles told him to tell me not to forget that Miss Connie wanted me to go meat and grocery shopping for her next weekend. Pop taking the book from his hand and walking away saying, "Ok."

Pop came to the head of my bed. I was still sitting up. He just stood there looking at me for what seemed like an eternity, smiling, then walked over to the window and tore off the gift wrapping that was red with a white ribbon and bow, and threw them out of the window. Then he ripped the binding and threw that out of the window into the airshaft below, followed by hands full of pages until the book in its entirety lay destroyed in the filth at the bottom of the shaft. Still smiling he said, "I'll tell your cousin you said thanks," and he walked away and rejoined Charles and Goldie in the living room.

Cousin Charles told Pop that one day I was going to be someone great. Goldie said that what I really needed was my ass kicked more often, not some mother-fucking book. "His head is too full of shit as it is, cut the head off and the body will die." "Dick." "Just like a nasty, filthy, dirty, fucking snake." Goldie said. Charles wasn't smiling anymore. He asked, "Where's Del-li-roy?" That's how he pronounced Delroy. Pop said that he was in the back and called for him to come up front. I did not allow myself to cry. Sitting there, wet and cold, thinking just how beautiful the book was bound and the cover inlaid with gold print. How I would have loved flipping through its pages and dwelling upon Poe's every written word. No greater caring owner could it have had than I would have been.

Every word Poe had written was engraved in my memory, but to own them in fine print, now there was the prize and the wonder of it all. And he had deprived me of something as simple as the ownership of a book. Just because he knew that the act would hurt me. Sitting there in my own foulness I tried to hate him but found still that I was absent of that emotion. I wanted to feel the relief that feeling the emotion hate would give me, the release. A stranger it remained however. All I could think about was how lovely the book was. And the razor and the mirror and the dull relief they could bring me. I despised me but could not hate them.

Crying, I suppose, would have brought some relief but the day was far too young and all had not yet arrived. There would be ample time for tears as the day progressed, and the evening lingered. For they had not yet finished the first fifth of booze, nor eaten dinner, nor had they sang 'Happy Birthday' and blown out the candles. No, the youth of the day had not yet matured into the anger of the night. The tears I would shed later would have to prove to be a brace to hold me up throughout the night. I have yet to make it to eight years and two days.

Delroy was making his way through the room and just as he got to the head of my bed, he started to sing 'Happy Birthday'. When he got to the part, "to you", he climbed onto the bottom bunk and yelled in my ear "To you!" Then he started to hum 'Happy Birthday' and yelled again "To you!"

He was dressed in a dark blue collarless suit with a white shirt with a Peter Pan collar and a light blue bow tie and navy blue shoes. On his head he wore the gold cardboard crown Pop had given him. I wanted to spit in his face but knew if I did, pop would kill me.

"You smell like piss," he said, "Wet, stink yellow piss." "We had home fries, fried apples, cheese eggs, rolls and a bunch of other stuff for breakfast." "What'd you have?" "Piss?" "What you gonna have for dinner, more piss?" "I know, strong, day old piss, on toast." I wanted to knock that smirk off of his face. Just push it into the back of his head with my fist. Letting the thought pass, I just told him to leave me alone. Pop had, during this exchange, put on a record, Errol Garner. Delroy hit me on top of my head, jumped down and said, "Gotta go, Bro," and ran into the living room. Pop yelled, "Hey Champ!" Goldie said, "Hit it Delroy!" Encouraging him to dance, Charles held out his hand saying, "Give me five, Del-li-roy," and Delroy gave him five, broke into a dance while cocking his crown to the left side of his head with his right hand, grinning from ear to ear. I thought to myself, you kiss ass.

Pop jumped to his feet and joined Delroy in his dance. He would then perform a dance step and Delroy would copy Pops dance steps, to the loud raving, delightful roars of Charles and Goldie. "That's your boy alright Dick." "Don't know where you got that other motherfucker from." "Get it boy, get it!" Goldie yelled while swallowing another drink and washing it down with ice cold Ballentine Ale. "Get it!" He yelled through clenched, pure perfect white teeth encircled by thinly formed lips laced by a shoestring mustache. He reminded me of an olive-skinned James Cagney with a loud dirty mouth, who would cut his mother if she pissed him off.

I always took great effort to stay out of his way. On that day I developed a profound dislike for Errol Garner and didn't listen to him again for years. Brook Benton, either, and every time I heard 'The Stroll', I smelled pee. The family members were now starting to arrive in two's and three's. The party was coming into its own.

In order to give you a clearer picture of who each person was and what part they played in my life, let me first describe them to you. The family patriarch was my father's uncle, my grandmother's brother, Herbert Reed. He was a short man, about five feet four inches in height, stocky in build. His hair was straight and thinning on top but well groomed. There was a missing tip off of his left index finger due to an accident that had occurred when in his younger years he had worked as a blacksmith. A man of very few words, but when he did speak his words were obeyed the very instant they were spoken.

Uncle Herbert smoked large cigars held tightly between his teeth in expensive cigar holders. When he talked you had to listen very carefully due to the mumbled effect caused by him never unclenching his cigar from between his teeth. And if you didn't understand him the first time you had better pretend you did. Getting it right the first time was of utmost importance. You see, Uncle Herbert didn't repeat himself and didn't tolerate mistakes and when it came to business, he was very unforgiving. A fair and non-judgmental man none-the-less, I thought he treated everybody the same.

You were below him, as long as you understood that, everything was just fine. Uncle Herbert, from what I knew of him, once owned a fleet of ice trucks. Talk was that he ran bootleg booze and beer for Dutch Shultz, and from time to time would hide some in his icehouse or in one of the many beach houses that he owned along the boardwalk in Far Rockaway. If you need a whore, see one of Mr. Herbert's people. If you want to play a number, you had to play with one of Mr. Herbert's boys. If you needed a bottle of something after hours, or on Sunday or on a holiday, you went to Mr. Herbert. Ran a little short on cash? Mr. Herbert was the person to see. There wasn't a card or dice game that could take place out on the Island unless Mr. Herbert gave his O.K, and one of Mr. Herbert's boys had to be there to cut the game. He had to make sure that he was getting his fair share. It was even said that Uncle Herbert got a cut of the Irish Sweepstakes. Was that true? I really don't know.

Even with all the wheeling and dealings that he was involved in, I knew one thing for sure, Uncle Herbert believed in Almighty God. Without fail, he went to church every Christmas and every Easter Sunday just like the good Christians of our present day America. In his role as Patriarch, Uncle Herbert made sure that every Easter each child in the family received an overstuffed Easter basket. There was a gift of cash for every child until he or she reached eighteen and he remembered all of our birthdays. Understand, dates are number's, number's were his business; Uncle Herbert never, ever, forgot a number or group of numbers.

He never, as I can remember it, spoke directly to me. He would always greet me by tapping me gently three times on my left shoulder with his left hand. I always enjoyed him touching me. Without fail I was always given a silver dollar. I always loved to walk from 'B' 68th street, on the Boardwalk all the way down to Rockaway Play Land Amusement Park. Along the way I would just enjoy the smells and sounds of life. He knew this about me and always slipped that silver dollar into my pocket. It was rare when I would spend it on anything for myself. I would always end up giving it to some poor person that I happened upon sleeping under the boardwalk or begging for food.

When at Uncle Herbert's I was free just like the waves that washed up on the shores of Rockaway Beach. I came and went as I pleased.

Even on rainy days I would frolic freely along the beach tasting the fresh, salty, misty air on my tongue. I would hold my eyes tightly closed and travel to better and friendlier places. No one ever tormented me at Uncle Herbert's house, no one, not even Pop.

Mom and Pop always made sure that I was extremely well groomed and that there were no visible marks on me whenever I was going to Uncle Herbert's. They always however warned me to keep my mouth shut and not to eat like they had not fed me. Most of the time they hadn't, but I was always good at pretending.

Uncle Herbert, for some reason always, I believe out of concern, prepared my meals or directed Aunt Jessie to do it. I was given the choicest cuts of meats. Rather than the wing, I was given the breast, and the entire leg. My plate was always piled high with food. Instead of a glass of something to drink, I was given a pitcher. It was a though he had some sort of insight into my plight. If he did, he never uttered a word aloud concerning the matter. Every moment that I spent in his company I cherished because I was allowed to feel human, normal and free and safe in a world that was not invaded by hate and pain. No turmoil.

There I had sweet sea breezes, clean clothes, and white sands between my toes. Sea shells that when held to my ear told me tales of their travels from far off lands and of their encounter with strange creatures that I had only read about or seen only in my dreams. Most of all, I always received three gentle taps on my left shoulder from the left hand of my uncle Herbert. And never once did I give any thought to the mirror and the razor.

Uncle Herbert had two sons, little Herbert and Dickie. Both were short men with almond skin and straight jet-black hair. Both of them handsome beyond words like their father. They had normal jobs but were in their father's business, each in charge of certain areas of the operation. I saw Dickie more than I did little Herbert, and I liked Dickie more. As far as I was concerned, Dickie was the master of cool and suave. He always had the finest of women. He always had a smile on his face and spoke in a very low, smooth, calm voice through his teeth. Word was that he was the most dangerous and deadly of them all.

Dickie served in the Navy during World War II. I would sit with him for hours while he told me stories of his adventures. He enjoyed talking to me because I knew how to listen with my mouth shut and learn without judging. What he didn't have was the power to protect me from the others.

My time spent with him was always pleasurable. Uncle Herbert also had two daughters, Elizabeth, called Tit, and Celestine, called Cel. Both were very beautiful women and I think that they both cared a little for me and showed it openly sometime. I never knew who their mother was, nor was I interested in asking. I don't know why, I just wasn't that interested in the dead. Next there was my father's uncle; Booker T. Reed Sr. He was about five feet ten inches tall, stocky and handsome.

His wife's name was Jessie, a beautiful woman who loved me deeply. They had one child; a son named Booker T. Reed Jr., his nickname was Junie. Junie was a happy child, always laughing, and a real joy to be around. I taught him how to ride a bike, even though I never learned myself, how to catch a ball, just how to be a boy. Junie was the brother that I dreamed of having, my chubby little teddy bear. He was a few years younger than I was and I protected him from all the harm that came his way.

Uncle Book, that's what the children in the family called him, was a quiet man who worked as a token clerk for the New York City Transit Authority: that was his legitimate job, on the side he ran the Harlem numbers operation up town. Beneath that quiet demeanor, he carried a stainless steel, pearl handled, snub-nosed .38 caliber pistol and reported to no one besides his brother, my Uncle Herbert. Uncle Book was a church going, fall down on his knees every morning and night and pray, family man. So he didn't deal in drugs, whores, and booze.

You could find him, Aunt Jessie and Junie in church every Sunday morning. He also enjoyed cigars, sometimes with a holder, sometimes without. His speech was very rapid, it kind of resembled Mumbles in the Dick Tracy cartoon (except with a cigar in his mouth). I always understood his every word. I guess it was because he always spoke kind and lovingly to me. Whenever and wherever he would see me he would always greet me with a smile and a hug. It was the same with Aunt Jessie; she was always hugging and kissing me.

There was always an open invitation for me to come spend the night at their apartment. There she would give me a nice hot bath, a clean pair of PJ's and underwear, all the food that I could eat and all the love and attention that I could stand. Never once out of the countless times that I stayed there did I ever wet the bed. Some evenings Aunt Jessie, Junie and I would go for walks in the park or just downstairs to sit on the bench in front of the building on a cool summer night.

One night when the Giants baseball team was home at the Polo Grounds, the three of us stood in the bedroom window looking right down through centerfield at Willie Mays. We drank Kool-Aid and ate Jiffy-Pop Popcorn, and just watched the game there from our pedestal in the sixth floor window of the projects.

Another time the three of us boarded the eighth avenue bus and rode off at twilight to the end of the line. I remember that as the bus made its turn to head back uptown my eyes got real heavy and I rested my head on Aunt Jessie's chest. She started to hum and the vibrations in her breast lulled me to sleep.

I felt protected in her and Uncle Book's care. I felt like I belonged to a family. It was Uncle Book and Aunt Jessie who provided my transportation to Far Rockaway. They would also take me on picnics and bus outings and boat rides around Manhattan. Whatever was normal for their son to do, they tried to make it a point to include me. The problem was that I always had to go back to reality. I always had to return home to where the mirror and the razor dwelled and waited gleefully for my return.

Now let me introduce you to the Matriarch of the family, Laura Reed Campbell, the eldest of the living children. Her siblings called her Sister or Lolla (pronounced Lol-la). She was pretty in a passing sort of way, darker than the others in both color and mood, old beyond her years. It was said that she was in constant contact with the dead. I have been in her company many a time when she would claim to spot some dead friend or relative moving in and about among the living.

Nobody in the family was allowed to die unless Aunt Lolla got the OK from the great beyond for you to pass over. If you left before then, well, it wasn't your time and you were doomed to wander the in-between forever. When you became ill, Aunt Lolla had to see you before the doctor could. If you were put in the hospital she had to be your first visitor. While in the hospital you could only eat the food that she prepared and bought to you. Believe me, Aunt Lolla would visit you everyday, three times a day and feed you every meal. When someone died it was Aunt Lolla that decided how you were going to be dressed, what color you were going to wear, where you were going to be buried and the kind of coffin you were going to be buried in. She even decided what the exact time your spirit left your body was and whether it was happy or angry. She even chose your last words for you, didn't matter whether she was there or not. If she said, that is what you said, then that is what you said, period, the end.

Cost was no problem, whatever Aunt Lolla wanted, Uncle Herbert and Uncle Book paid for it. Everybody in the family was put away nicely. Aunt Lolla also grieved the loudest, cried the loudest, and would faint the best, and she always volunteered to pass me over the dead to remove the dead person's evil spirit. She said I was the best choice since nobody liked me anyway. And that evil loved evil company, so the sprits of evil would be right at home inside of me. I was not allowed to look her directly in her eyes nor was I ever allowed to enter her bedroom, or any room in which she had fallen asleep.

I was not permitted to look at or touch a photograph of her, nor eat out of a plate that she had eaten out of, or drink from a glass that she had drank from. If I touched her when she was not looking, it brought about harsh punishment upon my person. She would make my father beat me until she had enough. Once the beating lasted an entire day. She allowed him to stop to rest for a few hours at a time. Another time she had him remove the mattress from the bed and tie me naked spread eagle and face down on the bed springs and beat me with the cord from the iron, just because I stepped over her outstretched legs. There were three different occasions when she had gotten drunk and started to laugh uncontrollably. She accused me of casting a spell on her and said that I had a powerful demon inside of me that gave me great power.

Of course I had no such power, but she said that in order to remove the spell and cast out the demon, the demon child had to be beaten with a black wire hanger doubled-over, struck seventy-seven times drawing blood with each stroke. The strokes had to be administered by a strong man, not a relative. My mouth was forced open as wide as it could be opened and a block of cider wood was forced into it. The wood served a dual purpose, one, it muffled my screams, two, it captured the demon when it tried to escape through my mouth. They also tied a royal blue cloth under my chin and over the top of my head. Royal blue was a holy color and it also held the block of cider wood in place.

I was stripped naked and my arms and legs were tied to the four corners of a doorway facing east. The cold and distant attitude of my mother still baffles me to this day. I still remember, as though it happened only moments ago, pleading and crying and begging her not to let them hurt me. But there never was a hint of emotion or affection on her face. The first blow landed, Wa-Splat! I attempted to scream and it came out as a high-pitched whistle that seemed to linger in the room forever. Searching through tear filled eyes; I found my mother's face. She hadn't even flinched. The expression on her face hadn't changed. Someone who was standing near by threw cold salt water on me, it burned. Someone else yelled, "No blood!" The room was filled with smiling faces, most were relatives, and some were strangers, others, friends of the family. Pop and Cousin Goldie were there too. Aunt Lolla was still laughing wildly. The strong man struck me again, Wa-Splat! "No blood!" someone yelled again. The cold salt water was thrown on me, burning once again like fire.

Through clouded eyes, I saw my brother Delroy standing next to my mother. She had her arm around his shoulder and his head was resting on her hip. He had a half smile on his face. I kept looking into my mother's eyes; mine were saying, "Please help me." Her eyes looked through me as though I wasn't there. Wa-Splat! "Got blood?" Cold saltwater splashed onto my bleeding back searing burning pain shot through me. I heard Goldie's voice call out from somewhere in my fog, "Kill the beast and the demon will die." Aunt Lolla began to laugh louder and began to roll on the floor. Wa-Splat! "Got blood?" The cold, burning salt water came again.

How many times the strong man struck me, I don't know. Sometime during the process I fainted. Was I struck seventy-seven times? I don't know. Maybe Aunt Lolla just stopped laughing. No one ever told me. That was the first time and I was only four years old. This torment I had to endure twice more before I reached nine years of age. Will I ever forget the total lack of concern or affection displayed by my mother for her child? I don't know. I haven't.

Who was the real beast and who truly is the demon? For now I have to take you back to the party. The others I will give you more details on as they arrived. The girls were now dressed and pretty and sitting in the living room. Mom was cooking the two large fresh killed capons the Pop had brought in with him that morning. She was also busy making candied yams and macaroni and cheese. On top of the stove, Pop was cooking a large pot of pig's feet and another pot of mustard and collard greens mixed together. It was going to be a wonderful birthday party that I was going to be present for, but not invited to.

Pop, on one of his trips to the kitchen to check on his pots or to get ice or beer, took a large quilt from the closet and draped it over the cross bar in front of my bed. The cross bar prevented me from rolling out of the top bunk during the night. He also sometimes used it as an instrument of punishment on me during his fits of rage. He attached the other two corners to two nails on the wall behind my bed, forming a makeshift tent. He did this, he said, so that company, while passing by, would not have to look at my nasty ass and fuck up their day. "I got this quilt fixed motherfucker, so if you try to move it to see what's going on, I'll know it." "I'll know it if you move it one fucking inch, and then I'll kick your stink nasty ass in front of everybody." You hear me?" "Yes, sir," I replied.

I lay there in the darkness with the fumes from my own urine burning my nostrils and eyes. There was no way that he could have fixed that quilt but I decided it would be best if I just played along. Maybe, just maybe, this time he would take pity on me and after the party was over and everybody had gone home, he would give me something to eat. I was so very hungry and everything smelled so good. The thought made my stomach growl loudly. For now what I wanted was to be as silent and as motionless as possible, invisible, and I didn't want to draw any attention to myself.

So I lay there as still as I could and listened to the people arrive and greet each other. They were singing along with the music eating snacks that made my mouth water. Drinking, dancing and laughing. Everyone was having a grand old time at my birthday party. From time to time people would walk pass me, but never giving me any notice. One person asked Pop upon returning to the living room, "Is that him under there?" Pop answered, "That's it." Cousin Goldie chimed in "Should be dirt covering his ass, not a damn blanket," the remark was followed by a chorus of laughter. I did everything I could to fight back the tears. There was little fight left in me so the tears flowed like water down a rainspout during a torrential downpour.

My eyes must have looked like I had just gone fifteen rounds with Sugar Ray Robinson with my hands down. My anus was raw and burning hot, as though my bowels were trying to push their way out. The newspaper was soaked with blood, urine and pus, and was falling apart and needed to be changed. The ink from the newspaper was going to cause a greater risk of infection. Moving when ordered not to would bring on the risk of a whipping. Staying put seemed the wiser choice.

Mom was dressing while cooking, seeming not to care at all that all the money that Pop had spent on this festive occasion more than likely came from the pocketbook of the woman he slept with last night. She was just as happy as a lark, cooking and primping. Forgetting that last night she and her children had to eat government corned beef, potatoes and white bread washed down with tap water. Now today they were eating like royalty, fat on the hog. It was more likely than not that his mistress was sitting there in her living room right now sipping on a gin and tonic and would be introduced to her as a close friend of the family's or his cousin.

Mom was going to laugh, dance, eat, party, and have a good time anyway. "Hey bro!" That sounds like Aunt Mattie I said to myself as in the confines of my darkness I lay. "Let's get this party started," the voice said. Pop responded "Sis, Eddie Lee." I was right, Mattie was Mom's baby sister and Eddie Lee was her boyfriend. They had been a couple for as long as I can remember. Eddie Lee was tall and very fair-skinned, chubby, well groomed and had a gold tooth. He had reddish brown hair that he wore in a flat top style haircut. A very jolly and kind man, as I recall who never treated me with ill regard. There was somewhat of an uneasy closeness between us that existed.

There was always this attempt on his part to do as much as he could for me without stepping on my father's toes. Eddie Lee would always intercede on my behalf when Pop was beating me. His easygoing manner had a calming effect on Pop, so he was always able to talk him down from his rage and anger or remove him from the area I was in. Now Mattie was a different story. She was pretty, slender and a college graduate. A party girl at heart, her nickname was Peaches, a name that applied to the smoothness and even tone of her olive brown skin. Her hair was beautiful, long and black. She usually wore it draped down over her shoulders with bangs crossed over her forehead.

Mattie loved to dance and was always the

life of the party. She could drink any man under the table and I never saw her stagger or drunk. She was always a lady. Mattie was a strong believer in education and pushed me to study hard and to read anything and everything that I could get my hands on. She didn't like me all of the time, why I don't know. What I do know is that if she could have provoked some form of punishment on me, she never did, whether real or imagined. I was always very careful around her because her moods concerning me were subject to rapid change if I carried myself in a manner unbecoming of a gentleman. Granted on the other hand, there was nothing she would not do to enhance my future on the educational and social level.

She taught me the value of being well versed in all aspects of life. She taught me how to be able to blend into any environment. What she did after greeting everybody in the living room was to ask, "Where's the birthday boy?" Pop said, "In his pissed up bed." Without responding to pop's comment, Aunt Mattie came into the bedroom and walked over to the head of my bed.

She said, "Nephie, Nephie you awake?" I said, "Yes Aunt Mattie, I'm awake." "You sound like you've been crying, have you?" She asked. I said, "No, I'm just thinking." "What are you thinking about?" She whispered, "Tell Auntie in her ear." I said, "I can't." "Aunt Mattie wants to give you a happy birthday kiss ok?" "Ok," I said.

She slid the quilt aside and jumped back, "What happened to your face, Bobby?" "You've been crying." "Crying," I said, "No, no, no Auntie I haven't been crying, I've been thinking and sleeping, just thinking and sleeping that's all, honest." I begged, "Please don't tell my father that I've been thinking and sleeping so hard, promise, promise." "I promise Bobby, happy birthday nephie, happy birthday." She kissed me and walked back into the living room.

Pop asked, "What's he doing?" Aunt Mattie said "He's sleeping Bro, sleeping." And he laughed. Aunt Mattie just said, "Come on Bro, let's dance." Aunt Mattie knew that Pop would have tormented me more if he knew that I was upset.

This was the one-day that she was not going to allow him to make me the object of his ridicule. She must have sensed something else was more terribly wrong, a deeper pain, pain that I did not know how to express or was ashamed to. Aunt Mattie had her Master's in social sciences and worked with young boys with emotional problems. She knew something very different happened to me. I was changed forever.

Auntie also knew that here was not the place to address the issue. Knowing what she did of me, that the moment she walked away the opportunity was forever lost. The secret would forever be sealed deep within me, in my hiding place, the hiding place where I keep all my other horrors, and all of my other pains. So what Aunt

Mattie was doing was dancing Pop around an issue like all other issues concerning me, he would only make them worse. As I have already told you, Aunt Mattie loved to dance, and she was a good dancer.

"Boo-boo, boo-boo, come on now, give your aunt just a little more in her glass." "Aunt Agnes." I said to myself, begging for more booze but already drunk on her butt. Agnes Reed Bryant, baby sister to Uncle Herbert and Uncle Book, Pop's aunt. I don't remember her ever holding down a job. She drank a lot, was a chain smoker that exhaled through her nose and her boyfriend Mr. Bob, who I won't go into detail about because of his unimportance, beat her.

Excessive drinking had taken its toll on her body but she was still a striking beauty, tall for a woman of the day, about five foot seven. She had long flowing black hair, copper-toned skin that never needed make-up. Her choice of drink was whatever you were serving but would buy mostly Sneaky Pete cheap wine for her self with her welfare check. Aunt Agnes called everybody Boo-boo and was normally kind and gentle when sober. There was this one time though when she accused me of looking up her dress and kicked me in the face. She had gotten so drunk that she forgot that she was wearing slacks and penny loafers. The loafers were new and she asked me to put new shiny pennies in them for good luck. I was devastated; we were at my father's mother's house across the street from Mount Morris Park.

After she kicked me in the face, I ran across the street and into the park. I found a piece of broken glass, went into the park bathroom, looked into the dirty mirror and began to cut into my face. Oddly, rather than find comfort that day I only inflicted pain. I found out that day that comfort for me only came from the mirror and the razor at home. After that day, I never looked at Aunt Agnes the same again. Not her or any other person who was a drunk. Yes, I learned that day that comfort and relief from my pain came from only gazing in my own special mirror and using pop's razor.

For me to describe to you the emotions that overtook me is even today impossible. There were no inner voices calling to me. No overwhelming desires. It was more like a hunger pang that just had to be satisfied whenever something, or someone, hurt me. What I was doing was removing or cutting myself out of the picture. All that was wrong was being cut away so that something right could grow back in its place. That way, everything would be all right and nobody would hurt me anymore. And maybe, just maybe, I would grow into something beautiful.

I never cried when I went about the task and I never felt any pain. There really weren't any spoken words either. What I would do was cut, and say, softly, "Ouch!" Mournfully, I would just say "Ouch!" Not because it hurt when I cut myself, no, not at all, I just hurt so much inside that saying "Ouch, Ouch, Ouch!" Over and over again, was an emotional release from my inner pain, my torment. It helped me feel a little bit less empty; never did it satisfy the hunger. It was like giving a starving man a soda cracker, only enough to make him want more, not enough to take away the hunger pang. Not enough to sustain life. Much to ponder for a child of eight years and one day you might say. Ponder deeply I did.

Able to cope was I, due to a lot of help from friendly and caring human intervention of others that saw my plight. Two of whom have already arrived. They were a mother and daughter who lived in our building one flight up and to the rear of our apartment building, Mrs. Margaret, and her daughter Vivian Beckford. Mrs. Margaret was a heavyset, very vocal, well-respected proper woman who sometimes walked with a cane due to a severe arthritic condition that she laughingly referred to as Uncle Arthur.

Mrs. Margaret was always dressed in mink coats, fox stoles, and Persian lamb coats. She was a class act who did not tolerate bad speech or behavior from anyone, and everyone in the neighborhood knew and respected her. I on the other hand knew and loved her. She was one of my special people because she treated me like a special person.

It was important to her that I pronounce certain words a certain way. Words like issue, bath and schedule. Mrs. Margaret taught me to stride rather than simply walk. She said, "Animals walk, men stride and women glide." Another important thing that she taught me was you are only as poor as you think you are. "Wealth begins with effort and ends in accomplishment." She often said. The most lasting and important of all things that she taught me was that beatings give momentary pain, conversation gives everlasting love.

It was sad that I received this wisdom and encouragement mostly after Pop had beaten me, and my visit with the razor and the mirror and the razors work had already been accomplished. She, none-the-less, has left a lasting impression on my life. Even then she would save me on many a morning from my father's rage.

Mrs. Margaret would be walking down the hallway on her way to work and hear the beginning of my beatings. She would knock on the rear door with her cane and yell, "Mr. Dickerson, open the door I want Bobby to go to the store for me!" Pop would stop mid attack and open the door smiling and say "Come on in Mrs. Margaret." Mrs. Margaret would barge right in, walk directly into Mom and Pop's bedroom and sit on the foot of their bed and ask my mother "What's going on in here?" Mom would remain silent. Pop would attempt to explain. "He pissed in his." Before he could complete his sentence Mrs. Margaret would cut him off, "He what?" "And I wasn't talking to you, was I?" "Does anything come out of that hole in your face that isn't filthy?" "I'll ask you again Mrs. Dickerson, "What's going on in here?" Mom very sheepishly said, "Bobby wet his bed again and Leroy was spanking him, that's all." Mrs. Margaret replied, "Mrs. Dickerson, that wasn't a spanking that was a beating, I could hear his cries all the way upstairs." "It sounded like he was hitting a side of beef." "Mrs. Dickerson, look at your baby, he's bleeding."

Mom continued to look at the floor while Mrs. Margaret was talking to her. Mrs. Margaret, placing two of her fingers under her chin and lifting and tilting Mom's head toward me said, "Mrs. Dickerson, one day he's going to kill that baby because you won't do anything, do you understand me?" Mom was looking at me but as always she didn't see me. She was looking with glazed eyes right through me. For her I wasn't really there nor had I ever been.

Pop broke the momentary silence, "Mrs. Margaret, you live upstairs and you don't know what really goes on down here." "You don't know what it's like having to raise a child that no school will take and having a little fuck that knows shit and nobody knows how in the fuck he knows it." "He knows shit that college kids don't know." "But he lies up in my mother-fucking house, eating up my mother-fucking food, wearing my mother-fucking clothes, and pissing in my mother-fucking bed." "It's just like my aunt and the rest say, he's a fucking witch, a fucking demon, and if he won't die, sooner or later I'm going to kill his ass and go to jail for it."

"You can't be here all the time." Mrs. Margaret shook her head and said, "See how ignorant you are?" "This innocent child is a gift from God, not a demon." "If you and your brow-beaten wife weren't so stupid you would see that." You couldn't even speak in one paragraph without being vulgar." "Bobby, wrap a towel around you and go upstairs to Vivian." "Tell her that I said to dress your wounds and give you a bath."

"Then, she's to fix you some fried chicken and waffles for breakfast before she leaves for school." "No, tell her to stay home with you today, and Bobby, don't come back here until I get home tonight." "I want you safe today, do you understand me?" Pop said, "You can't do that, he's my son." "He's your punching bag!" Mrs. Margaret said, "Now get out of my way or I'll split your head open with this cane." "Now run Bobby, run upstairs."

Pop moved out of the way, and wet and bleeding, I ran barefoot down the hallway and up the one flight of wooden stairs to Mrs. Margaret's apartment door and knocked once. In an instant Vivian opened it and said, "I know, I heard what was going on through the airshaft." Hell, the airshaft was better than a telephone in those days.

Maybe it was the relief of being safe or the joy of seeing Vivian. I can't remember which, but

I broke into tears, not just crying, but also sobbing. It was like someone had opened the floodgates of my emotions and everything that I had been holding in came pouring out. Vivian cradled me in her arms and guided me into the apartment. She felt warm and smelled good and I felt safe.

Vivian was older than I was by about eight years. Very attractive with a shape that made Dorothy Dandridge look like Olive Oyl and I had a very bad crush on her with designs on making her my wife once I had grown into manhood, not really though, it was just childish thinking and hopefulness. In the wishful thinking of a child, I thought that if I married Vivian, she and Mrs. Margaret would always be there to protect me from the ills of the world.

Maybe one day Vivian would let me kiss her on the lips and she would get pregnant and have a baby boy that we would name Bobby Jr. And we would never beat him and he would never wet the bed, and we would be happy and Mrs. Margaret would live forever. Of course you could not get a girl pregnant by kissing her on the lips and no one lived forever. And without a doubt, who can really protect you from all the ills of the world? Life isn't that simple. The idea of what the future might hold was refreshing and was worth holding on to for the moment. For now the moment was divine.

Vivian ran me a bathtub full of warm soapy water and took off my dirty rotten yellow wet under clothes. I eased into the water because the soap burned my open sores. She winced with me then smiled a little saying, "It's alright Bobby, don't worry, I won't hurt you." The water was soothing and like Vivian, smelled of Tea Rose. She softly ran the washcloth over my shoulders and back allowing the water to trickle gently over the welts and bruises that laced my neck and upper body. Each time she touched me, she would say almost in a whisper, "I am so sorry baby, I am so sorry." Her eyes were welling up with tears and I didn't want her to cry so I just kept telling her that it didn't hurt, even though it did.

When I stood, Vivian could no longer hold back the shock or the tears. She saw that one of my testicles had been pushed up into my groin, by my father` during one of my beatings Vivian discovered. It was very painful as she washed the area. There were also a large number of scabs over infected wounds on my legs, thighs and hips that had gone unattended to. She started to cry and ran from the bathroom. I stood there for a moment in wonderment not understanding at first what the problem was. For me, the way I was, was normal.

Then I came to the realization that for her it wasn't and I felt ashamed and I finished washing and dried off with the clean, soft towel that was there on the towel rack for me. Vivian had placed my dirty underclothes in the sink in some soapy hot water to soak and had in their place left me one of her nightgowns and a robe.

I put them on and walked out into the kitchen where she was standing, mixing waffle batter and still crying. When she saw me she turned her back toward me and said, "Young men shouldn't let a lady see his nakedness you know, that's why I left." I said, "I know." Even though I knew the truth I decided it best to allow her to maintain her dignity.

Vivian was also frying some chicken. While fixing breakfast she directed my attention to a book on the table saying, "I am reading that for school it's by O'Henry. There's a short story in there that I want you to read, it's called," "The Last Leaf." "But first I want to dress those sores while the chicken is cooking Ok?" I said, "Ok," and we proceeded to go into the living room where she had laid out everything that she was going to need. In the living room I lifted the gown and she applied hydrogen peroxide, first aid cream, gauze and tape to the wounds on my legs. She repeated the same procedure on my back and shoulders. She was more affected by my condition than I was. I was so used to it by now it didn't bother me. I, being so unused to such loving care, was embarrassed by the tender light caring touching.

When she was finished I settled in at the kitchen table and began to read The Last Leaf by O'Henry. Vivian continued to cook the chicken and make the waffles. The story was very touching. It was about a girl that was sure that she was going to die when the last leaf fell from the tree that was located outside of her window. It never fell, because an old man, who was a painter, and who was later found dead, had climbed up and painted a picture of the leaf on the wall in front of her window. Love of the girl drove him to do it and cost him his life, "A loving story and beautiful but sad ending." I said to Vivian, "You know, Vivian, I would do that for you." She smiled at me and said, "Bobby you would do that for anybody." "Come on let's eat." We ate the fried chicken, waffles smothered in butter, and syrup. Then we got under the covers and read and talked the day away.

When Ms. Margaret got home from work, I went downstairs and knocked on the door. Pop opened the door without saying a word. I walked in and proceeded to go into my bedroom. That's when I felt the impact of his foot in my back and heard him say, "Did you think I wasn't going to kick your ass when you got home Motherfucker?" And he beat me. After he beat me and before I crawled into my still wet bed. I visited the mirror and the razor. They were happy to see me home again.

Pop wasn't very happy at all to see Mrs. Margaret and Vivian there, but was very unwilling to show his displeasure in front of company. So he greeted them as though they were long lost relatives. "Hey, glad you came down." "Have something to eat." "Get a drink, have a seat." "Make yourself at home." "Everybody, this is Mrs.

Margaret and Vivian Beckford, our neighbors from upstairs." "Mrs. Margaret is just like a mother to me and Annie. They looked at each other in a rather confused manner. Then in turn spoke to everyone as they were introduced. They asked where I was. Pop lied and said I was in the back somewhere and that I should be up soon. I wanted to yell out that I was in a makeshift tent being secluded from everything that was going on, but knew better, so I remained silent. Mrs. Margaret said, "Well," "I'll just go on in the back and see him because I have something for him." Pop jumped up. "No!" "He's on punishment." "I'll get it to him." "What is it?" "Some love you idiot." "Something I don't think you know how to give him." "Now, where is he?" As if on queue the music stopped and the living room went silent.

Mrs. Margaret and Vivian came into the bedroom and saw the makeshift tent and asked, "Is he under there?" They continued. "I don't believe what you are allowed to do to this child." "There has got to be a law somewhere that will protect him." Vivian pulled the quilt away and started to scream "Momma look, Momma look." "He is lying in a puddle of urine and there's blood everywhere." In an instant the room was crowded with people. So many people were talking at once that it was hard for me to understand who was saying what. Pop was yelling for every body to get back into the living room, and for Mrs. Margaret to get the fuck out of his house and to mind their own fucking business.

Mom was telling me that I had messed up the day for everybody just like always. "What did you do to yourself?" She asked. Crying I said. "Nothing, Mommy I haven't done anything." Vivian told Mom that if she didn't take me to the hospital, she was going to call the police. Pop said that they would change my sheets and take me in the morning and that he wanted them to leave right now. Mrs. Margaret, Vivian, Eddie Lee and Aunt Mattie decided to leave but warned Pop not to touch me or they would contact the police. And Mrs. Margaret informed Mom that she was going to check on me later that evening to make sure that Pop did not inflict any further punishment on me after she and the others had gone.

Mom said that I had probably done something to myself just to get some attention. And if I had I deserved whatever punishment was coming to me. "What kind of mother are you?" Mrs. Margaret asked. "That would allow this to happen to her child?" Pop told her to take care of her own and not to worry about his. They left and the makeshift tent remained and my sheets weren't changed. Mom told me that Pop was going to take care of me later for what I had done. Cousin Goldie told Mom that she should have let him cut my throat when he wanted to, that way they wouldn't have a problem to deal with now.

He said, "Shit doesn't stink unless you leave it lying around," "Shits in there now, just laying around." "Know what I mean Annie?" Mom replied, "It's just a little bit of shit Goldie, just a little bit of shit." "We can just wipe it up a bit later on tonight, Leroy and I." "You know what I mean?"

I knew what she meant. They were going to beat the heck out of me again. He was going to do it when he was so drunk that no matter where he hit me it wouldn't matter to him, nor would it matter with what. And she was going to help him gag me and was going to hold me down. Mrs. Margaret and Vivian would never hear the pain and torment that I was going to endure that night. It was going to be a night of horrors, this I knew. I had been through them before. Fear and dread were now my bedfellows and we waited in the darkness of my wet and smelly makeshift tent for the end of my birthday party, which was still not in full swing and all had still not yet arrived.

The music was back on and I was the topic of conversation for a few moments more, mostly about how Mom and Pop should send me away somewhere. Uncle Book, Aunt Jessie, Ms. Florence, Ms. Perry, Mr. & Mrs. Hicks all arrived at the same time. Besides Uncle Book and Aunt Jessie the others are really of no importance. They were just people that came in and out of my life at different times playing very minor roles in it.

My grandmother had also arrived. Delroy was her pet and whatever he wanted he got when ever he wanted. Her name was Lula Edith

Dickerson, my father's mother, one of the coldest people that I had ever met when she wanted to be. I had never seen her show any type of affection toward Pop. She was very light skinned, almost passing for white. With auburn hair that was shoulder length. She was very short, four feet nine inches tall. And thin with very tiny feet and thick eyeglasses. Not long after Pop's birth she ran off to New York from South Carolina for reasons that are still unknown to me. Pop called Granny, our name for her, Doeda (pronounced, Doe-da), why, I don't know. I never asked.

She hated dark-skinned people except for her live in boyfriend, Mr. Taylor. Who was blue-black and bore a very close family resemblance to King Kong. He hailed from Hollywood, Florida, could not read but could count money with the best of them. He worked everyday but I never knew what he did for a living. Mr. Taylor was always dressed to the nines, sharp as a brand new tack and he despised me. But like my grand mother, he loved Delroy.

Our relationship was strange. Some might say abnormal. Every two weeks I did all of their grocery shopping for them. They never struck me nor did they ever file a false report against me in order to get some form of punishment imposed on me. Granny did not allow Pop to go overboard and become brutal when inflicting punishment either. She would permit a smack or a few swipes on my buttocks or legs and that was it. She always bought me the best of everything, just like she did for Delroy. It was Mom and Pop who would take the gifts that she brought for me and give them to Delroy. Still Granny never kissed or hugged me, never. It always hurt me deeply because she couldn't seem to keep her hands off of Delroy. Always sitting him on her lap and stroking his hair.

She never allowed anyone to sit or lay on her bed. But whenever we were there at her house she would always send me across the street to Mount Morris Park to play so that Delroy could lie down in her bed and take a nap undisturbed. If Delroy did not feel like watching television, it didn't get turned on. If he did, I had to watch what Delroy wanted to watch and I had to watch in silence.

Upon arriving home I sought comfort in the mirror and from the razor. The sounds of laughter grew ever louder. Friends and family danced and partied to their hearts content. The sounds of Roy Hamilton singing "Get Happy and Jump for Joy" rang out. Ella Fitzgerald singing "All of You" and "Night and Day" filled the air along with Joe Williams "I'll Never Smile Again" and "A Man ain't Supposed Cry." The men and women held each other closely as they danced to "I Wish" by the Platters and hand danced to "Ain't Misbehavin" by Nat King Cole and I cried as I sang quietly along with Arthur Prysock when they played "For Your Love."

What a grand time they were having. The food smelled good. One by one they passed me with loaded plates. Each sitting and eating with their plates on their laps. My small empty stomach was churning and growling. The desire to beg began welling up inside of me, but the fear suppressed it. I was resolved to savor the aroma of those tasty morsels that I longed to have. I tried to concentrate on the music. What I didn't want to think about was what was going to happen after the party was over. What I tried not to dwell on was my immediate need to use the bathroom. So no longer able to hold it, I released myself and let the urine flow. As the hot fluid flowed out of me and into the already existing puddle, I thought. What does it matter? I am already wet. Nobody will know the difference.

I felt a hand reach under the quilt and touch me on the head I knew the touch. It was Aunt Jessie. She said, "Hi darling, happy birthday." "Here's something from Uncle Booker T. and me." She stuck some money in my hand and walked away. I didn't know how much she had given me at the time but found out later that it was ten dollars. When she gave it to me, I thought, this will buy us some food next week. Junie came next and stuck a drumstick under the covers but I handed it back because I had no way of getting rid of the bone, and if I had gotten caught with it Pop would have punished me more severely. Junie said, "I'll try to bring you some bread and ham," but he never came back.

Each time I moved, the urine would slosh about under me on the rubber sheet. The discomfort that I was experiencing is indescribable, wet, raw, and burning, all the feelings and sensations occurring at the same time. To say that I was even being considered as an object, by my mother and father, would be an overstatement. Others from time to time would make inquiry as to whether or not I was to be fed, but were ignored or put off with a comment like, "He'll eat later," or "His mother is going to feed him in the back," knowing full well that the intent was not to feed me at all. You have no idea how badly I wanted some red rice and ham and potato salad, it had been two days since last that I had eaten, except for the plaster that I had taken from the wall.

My heart beat slowly and softly then pounded, as it tried to decipher what move was suitable for the moment. In my tent I could not see the world around me, I could only feel, hear and smell all that was taking place. Some of Delroy's friends from the block and school had showed up too. Ronald and Donald (the twins), Butchie, Fhinie, Glenn, Ronald "A" we'll call him, Leroy, Tracy, Allen Ray, Wally. None of them played with me because they thought I was strange. When they picked teams for stoopball, stickball or basketball I was either not chosen or the last to be picked. Or if we were playing the guys from another block and were losing they would replace the worst player with me if a homerun or a touch down was needed to put the team on top.

I was a natural athlete with better than average speed and exceptional balance. I had been in a least one-fist fight with all of them and won. Once they had fought me they didn't want to try me a second time. So they used isolation, taunts, and rejection as their weapons. When I would go to the store it was usually at a run. This way I could avoid being teased by them. They were always at their bravest when in a group. I ran everywhere and could run for miles at a time. They called me names like, Mister Pee-body, and pissy-issy. Delroy would be the ringleader most of the time. If they had known what the man with the large eye had done to me I would never have lived it down. The thought of them knowing made my body quiver all over.

We spent a lot of our time at a park and basketball court located on 129th street on Eastside drive. There was also a baseball field there too. We called the park, "Down the Hill" because the street between Park Avenue and Lexington Avenue was at a slight incline. Most of the time however, we played basketball in front of a vacant lot between the rectory at All Saints Church and Butchie's building number 57 east 129th street. We hung a backboard and rim from the top of the fence. Rather than go down the hill to play baseball we would sometimes play stickball in the street or softball on the cement baseball field at elementary school 133 located on 131st street and Madison Avenue.

Often we would also pass the day away playing stoopball. During my youth there was very little traffic flow through 129th street. So when we played stickball, home plate was a manhole cover located about mid-block. We drew in second and third base with paint and it lasted throughout the summer months. The sticks or bats were made from old broomsticks of different sizes. You would decorate the grip end with tape. It also prevented it from slipping from your hands when you swung it.

The ball, well the ball had to be a pink Spalding, they were the best. The game was played just like baseball except because the ball was made of rubber you didn't have to use a baseball glove. The same rules applied for stoopball. The only difference being was that you threw the ball at the edge of the step. Then depending on the angle at which it struck it, the ball would either pop up or turn into a ground ball. Butchie's stoop was the most suitable for playing stoopball. It had a wide entranceway and only three steps. The stoop was home plate and we used chalk to draw in second and third bases. First base was a manhole cover.

Most of the time, the big guy's would join in and play with us. The girls were always hanging around watching us play and rooting us on. If they weren't downstairs they would watch us play from their windows. The adults were always very supportive and took an active part in our activities. The men would be the umpires and the women would sometimes fix us sandwiches and Kool-Aid if we had a big game over at 133rd or down the hill.

Freddie, one of the big guys in the block, who had taken me under his wing at an early age and helped me become an accomplished athlete, would always go with us to coach and maintain order during the games. It was because of him that I was able to catch a ball like Willie Mays, steal bases with the speed of Jackie Robinson and never was un-sportsman like in my conduct. If we won the game it was fine, if we lost the game so what, the next time we tried harder.

Freddie always picked me to be on his team, and I loved him because he was a straight up guy. He never taught any of the younger guys how to do anything wrong. Nor did he teach you Freddie's way. What he taught was the right way. The big guys in the block were Freddie and Rufus; they were brothers, Winston, Clyde, Brother, Milton and Elroy. All of them were cool with me.

They would always let me hang around them when I didn't have anybody to play with. Mostly they liked playing chess with me, or just talking to me because as Freddie once put it, "You're a fascinating little dude Bobby." Brother and Milton thought that I was heavy mentally. Winston, Clyde and Elroy used to pay me twenty-five cents a week to do their math homework. It is important that you understand that these guys were in high school and I was six, seven and eight years old, but seventy five cents was seventy five cents and it went a long way back then. The bonus, the real import of it all, was the respect that these older guys had for me and me for them.

If I had told Freddie what the fat man with the large eye had done to me he would have beaten him to within an inch of his life. Freddie, however, being a young man of honor, would have felt morally obligated to tell my parents. Please, understand why I choose not to tell Freddie either. Maintaining one's Honor and integrity was something else that Freddie Quinn taught me. It would have been dishonorable on his part if he had not informed my parents concerning the raping of me by the fat man with the large distorted eye.

Freddie and Rufus had two other brothers and a younger sister whose name I can't remember. The brothers' names were Butch and Billy. Billy we called Big Bill because though he was the same age he was larger than we were. He and I fought at least once a week. Then there was Butch and Larry Jackson, Tracy Swan, (I called him blackbird), and Jeffery Richardson, Michael Heath and Mac Roseburg, Fhenie's brother, the crew, the boys from 129th street between Madison and Park. For the most part all were pretty much kids from decent families who required of them a certain moral code. All were friends of Delroy's. None were friends to me, except for the big guys, who looked out for me.

All were there at the party that was supposed to be for the children but was headed at a very rapid pace toward a party for adults. The children were there mostly for entertainment. Delroy, being the main source of entertainment, was kissing up as he always did, competing with the others to be the center of attention, and putting on his innocent act in order to reap monetary rewards for just being cute.

I can remember one Christmas Mom, Delroy and I went to visit her parents in Alberta, Virginia. All of our young cousins were there along with our uncles and aunts on my mother's side of the family. As to details concerning them I won't be giving you any, except for two or three whom I will introduce to you later.

Anyway, on that Christmas morning we got up and ate a good down home on the farm country breakfast. My grand mother announced that it was time to open the presents that were under the giant decorated evergreen tree that was standing in all its festive glory in the parlor. My mother's, sister's daughter opened one of her gifts first. It was a large package in beautiful wrapping with a large yellow bow and ribbon. Inside was an "Easy Bake Oven". Needless to say she was happy beyond words.

Next her brother opened his gift, which was also beautiful to gaze upon. There, inside was a Davy Crockett suit complete with a coonskin hat.

He too was overjoyed. They both almost at the same time said, "Thank you Big Ma and Big Daddy." They smiled and Big Ma said, "Anything for Big Ma's lovely grandchildren."

Then it was decided that Delroy and I would open ours together since we were running late for church. What we found under the tree with our names on them were two brown paper bags with a red bow tied around them. I opened my bag first. There inside was an apple, a box of raisins, an orange and twenty-five cents. I respectfully thanked them and sat down.

Then Delroy opened his, broke into tears ran over to Big Ma and Big Daddy and hugged and kissed them. Big Ma said "Yes baby," "it's all right." "I know you're happy." She and Big Daddy kissed him and he came over and sat next to me on the chair. I leaned over and whispered in his ear, "Why do you always have to kiss ass?" "There's fucking fruit on the table."

I didn't realize it until it was too late that my mother had heard me. She back handed me in my mouth and called me ungrateful, which I wasn't. I was simply pointing out to Delroy that he was a kiss ass and that Big Ma and Big Daddy showed that they favored our cousins over us. Man! Ray Charles could have seen that. Delroy never seemed to mind kissing up or making a clown of him-self as long as he got what he wanted out of demeaning himself. Sometimes it was just a little extra attention or something as simple as an extra teaspoon of sugar on his corn flakes. So it was at the party. He would dance and the guest would throw coins at his feet like he was an organ grinders monkey. For the most part I was ashamed for him. I was ashamed because he was so willing to do just about anything for a few coins and to gain the favor of men.

For me it didn't diminish my pride at all to have to sweep out butcher shops and grocery stores or to search trashcans for soda bottles in order to cash them in for the deposit nor was I lacking in pride when I shined shoes or carried groceries at the A&P supermarket. It wasn't setting my self above the rest when I sat on the edge of a windowsill six story up in order to wash them for three cents a window using vinegar, water and newspaper to remove the soot of the city from them.

What I refused to do, without reservation, was demean who I was as a person. I would not dance and grin for you in order to make a dime and to gain your favor. On the other hand, for two dollars I would take your shopping list and do all of your grocery shopping for you. I would buy your Sunday news and coffee for you on any given morning. I would walk your dog for just five cents. Walk and give him a bath for a dime. If you needed someone to baby-sit for you, I would do it for twenty-five cents an hour. The price included diaper changes and feedings if you wanted me to care for an infant. Need your floors washed and waxed? Call me and on my hands and knees I would scrub your floors and supply the wax for fifteen cents. I always used DAN-DEE floor wax because it made the floors look like they were coated with glass but not leave them slippery.

My days, including weekends, were always filled with hard work and right-hearted things to do. What I did, I did for my family so that they did not have to go without all of the time, and I maintained my pride and dignity, because I didn't steal I from anyone nor did I ever con anyone out of anything. Not working hard would have been out of character for me. It would have been easy to just wait outside of one of the candy stores and steal all of their papers and make all of the profit. But of what benefit would that had been for me if I had gotten caught. No one would have ever trusted me again. And besides, honest money always, as far as I was concerned, spent better.

Looking over my shoulder was not how I wanted to live my life. Pop once beat me for three consecutive days for telling Mom that he had taken five dollars from her pocketbook. This was money that she set aside to pay the rent at the end of the month. Anyhow, the beatings never swayed me from telling the truth. If she had not asked if anyone had seen somebody go into her pocketbook I would not have told. When she did, I found that I was obligated to tell the truth. Delroy saw what happened to the money but lied and said that he hadn't. Pop rewarded him for keeping his mouth shut and not dropping a dime on him. Me, he called a ratfink. I never saw the benefit in his actions since it was the family as a whole that suffered because of what Pop had done. It was the family that was almost evicted for lack of five dollars in rent money when Leo the Landlord came to the door on the first of the month to collect.

It, as I can remember, was Mom who stood there barring the door so Mr. Leo could not gain entry and searching for an explanation as to why, again, she was short with the amount due. While Pop was off either drinking or gambling away a roof over the heads of his wife and children, here I lay rejected again for doing what was right for her, and still being punished rather than rewarded for it. If it were at all possible for me to escape this day by turning myself into another form or a puff of smoke, I would not have had to bare so much at so young an age. It was really far more than I could, at times, tolerate.

What I did was pretend well. And suffer greatly in silence. The silent suffering was what was taking a toll on my mental frame of mind. There was, in my life at the time, no other human that I could confide in. No friend into whom I could find total escape. No friend to whom I could pour out my entire soul. This too was a longing deep within me. Yet another prayer gone unheard, gone unanswered like all the rest. Still my only friend and companionship was the mirror and the razor, the burning sting, the cutting and pleasure. Only the sight of my bloody face afterward brought me a somewhat pure form of comforting.

I lay there in blissful desire and longing. Knowing full well that in the morning all the dirty dishes and glasses will be waiting for me, with their dried, greasy, remnants of what should have been a happy yesterday, in fact, only a prelude to all of my tomorrows. Awaking to rise to stark raving fear is what I had to look forward to. Smack! The sound made as Pop strikes out and hits me in the face and I fall back against the wall. It is hard for me to lie there, knowing, as I had learned the hard way that any act of defiance on my part would only result in more severe punishment. But defiance is what I decided to display and severe the beating I was willing to accept if it meant that he and they would only come to understand that I just don't want to be hit and beaten anymore.

What I pray is that they would understand, knowing what their walls of contempt for me would not allow, is that I cannot allow the tears of mock defeat to run freely and openly down my face in order to relieve them of their guilt or to make them satisfied with themselves after committing such brutal acts of abuse upon an innocent, just to rid him of some perceived evil that most surely existed more happily in them, than in me. Smack! I was again hit from behind, this time I was struck by a blow against my ear. I, in desperation, tried in vain to regain my composure and dodge his next blow, and the next, and the next, but was unable to.

"Fucking piss in my bed," "Fucked up my children's party," and you think that you can lie up in this piss with all these dirty dishes in the sink?" "You better get the fuck up or get fucked up," "You filthy, nasty, little son of a bitch." He screams into my ears. Pop continues to beat me as I topple in a clump to the floor. Laying there as Pop was kicking me and at me, running around in a rage yelling at me to sit up and follow him into the kitchen, each time I would try to rise he would either kick or punch me back into a fetal position.

Unable to respond verbally to his commands or to acknowledge that I understood something that he was ranting about, I simply nodded and responded as best as I could to every threat that he made. I waited for the chance when I would be able to breathe a sigh of relief. And somehow bring to the fore the will I would somehow need in order to survive another day. For the moment, though, just for the moment, I just didn't want to be beaten anymore. I didn't want him to hit me again. It wasn't the pain that he inflicted that bothered me. It was the pain and the agony of not knowing why he got such pleasure out of it. That is what tormented me so.

"Do the fucking dishes." Those words yelled at me awakened me from my day dreaming of an end to this terror and torment. Those words brought me back to reality. Those words and a swift hard kick to my lower back that impacted me so greatly that I thought that the soles of his shoe had cut and split the flesh just above my waist and the center of my back, as the pain distorts my childish features I hear Pop stomp off into the bedroom. I struggle to my feet and into the kitchen where the dishes awaited.

What he in fact had designated as a punishment chore was in reality a windfall, a reward of sorts, one might say. Leftovers, wonderful tasty leftovers from the party the night before, the plates were piled high with more food on them than could be eaten. And here I, I alone will get to savor the taste of food that had long been denied me. I proceeded to do what was best and logical for me to do. I consumed the remnants left on the bones of chicken legs and wings. The hard crust that had formed on the potato salad I scraped off and devoured the moist warmth of what was left behind. Dried candied sweet potatoes, and collard greens gone from hot to room temperature. Warm red rice hardened by exposure to the air, all proved to satisfy the hunger that had been raging inside of me. Careful I was though. I only ate as I scraped what was inedible into the garbage can. At times I would gag on a portion that had soured during the night or because I had filled my mouth to capacity and swallowing became impossible. Food picked over and leftover, but food none-the-less.

It's the way I had come to know, the way that

I learned to survive. Surviving had become harder than living. Each day of life proving to be a day more than I thought I could survive. I fed just like a wild beast that had not eaten but sparingly during the drought. Like the beast, I gorged myself on carrion left behind by another form of beast known to us a man. Pop always used food as a weapon of torture, and he knew that if he had thrown the leftover food in the garbage can, I would just dig out the good morsels and eat them anyway. He was never able to catch me.

I always, as quickly as I could, would cram my mouth full and with little chewing, swallow. Ash and cigarette butts would sometimes slow my pace because I would have to dig them out or carefully eat around the butts or the ash. Even when he would hock and spit into the garbage can as a means to deter me from seeking out its reward of food. I was able to sift about in the gore of it all for a few edible delights. There were tricks to my trade that Pop knew nothing about. His lack of knowledge is what I had depended upon to continue to survive.

There among the discarded edible delights was a slice of my birthday cake undefiled except for a discarded cigarette extinguished between the layers. In the short time that it took for me to consume it. I pretended for an instant that the cigarette butt was a birthday candle. And I ate the now dry and hardened morsel with a sense of joy and glee. "Happy Birthday dear Bobby, happy

Birthday to me," I sang to myself in silence as I went about my existence.

Humble,' though it was, and horrible as it was prone to be. I existed. So set about I did at doing the dishes. I had to continue to exist, to survive, to one-day escape to somewhere else besides the mirror. Escape to a place where comfort and pleasure resides in relief brought about by beauty and not the slash of a razor.

The sink is filled with hot soapy water. Halfway through the dishes I realized that I had forgotten to wash the glasses first. Then from behind me I heard my mother whisper in a voice she rarely uses with me, she said, "Bobby please," "please Bobby." "Wash the glasses." I turned and looked into her face and saw swollen red eyes. Her once, beautiful, shiny black hair, now dry and frazzled. She was wearing a frayed and un-ironed house smock with a row of safety pins lining her collar. As usual, she lacks make up. She is a broken woman. I know it and she knows it. Even to this day what I saw so long ago has become Mom's typical look. She has become that rumpled, dismayed, and subjective woman. Not happy, but conditioned, content to be just what she had become, a woman with a look of total hopelessness.

I nodded in acknowledgement of the advice that she gave me. In haste I began to wash the glasses. "Your father is going to want breakfast in a little while." She said. In a shuffle more than a walk she moved to her side of the bed and sat down on the corner at the head next to the window where on its sill she kept her ashtray and cigarettes, Kent's, king size in the soft pack. From there she would go off to where ever she goes when she doesn't want to be here. It was often that I wondered, does she think about me when she's gone?

I finished the dishes. Turned on the oven so that Pop could make toast and I place the two black cast iron frying pans on top of the burners of the stove. As the oven heated the roaches that had nested in its recesses began to stream out and up through the top burners. Turning on all four top burners blocked their escape and the odor of roasting roaches filled the air for a period. Once the heat and flames had done their jobs, you could cook in relative safety. If not done the roaches were prone to crawl about on the food as you cooked.

Alas, another condition that I wanted to escape from. Chores completed. I walked into Mom and Pop's bedroom right off of the kitchen. There I found myself standing directly in front of my mother. Still mind you in wet underclothes worn the night before and the night before that. Rank and wet I stood there battered and bloody from the punishment inflicted upon me by Pop and Mom and other family members, I stood there staring at her. I wasn't thinking about anything. There was just this uncontrollable desire, no compulsion, to just stand there and stare at her. I stood there for what seemed like forever. She seemed not to even notice me. Soon I got tired of staring and turned to move away.

Mom reaches out to me and draws me closer to her. She looks deeply into my eyes, leaning her head first to the left and then to the right as though she was seeing me for the very first time but having a memory of me from a very long time ago. "What's that above your eye?" She asks. Then a smile crosses her face. Then she examines my arms, legs, buttocks and shoulders.

Again she smiles, and asks. "Where did these come from?" Pointing at different wounds and bruises on my body and tracing the outline with her finger. Then with her right index finger, she starts to count the fine slash-like marks on my face. She is very thorough at and about her work. The bump on the left side of my head attracted extra attention. "This?" She asked softly. She knew that it had come from Pop slamming my head into the kitchen wall when I had not moved fast enough to please him. I knew that Mom really did not want me to tell her the truth. I always said what I was supposed to say, that I was injured playing tackle football at the park without equipment.

I stood clothed in only my wet underwear. And after she is satisfied that she has examined and recorded to memory all my marks and bruises she draws me close to her. Her arms engulf me and I am swallowed up in a wonderful warm embrace. I tell God, "Please don't ever let this end. I don't ever want her to let go." "God let me stay here in her arms forever." My eyes were held tightly shut, and for mere instants in time nothing else mattered. Mom pats my head and I flinch from the tenderness of the bumps and bruises Pop and Mom had inflicted on me that morning and in days past.

Mom then whispers in my ear, "If you ever say anything else, you know that your father will kill your nasty little ass." "Don't you?" "Now get the fuck away from me." Then she breaks the embrace, and goes back to where she was before, never land. I dress as fast as possible so that I could go out and make my Sunday money by shopping for the neighbors and getting the Sunday newspaper for others. Pop was in the living room listening to gospel music. Pop kind of leaned toward the Lord on Sunday mornings, even attending my Uncle Paul's church some Sundays. Pop and his cousins usually turned church attendance into an outing.

It was normal for them to keep a fifth of something in one of the cars. Off and on during the service, two at a time they would make their way out to the car to get a little hook, as they called a shot of booze or two. Before the service was over they were drunk, loud and extremely holy and touched by the Lord. At home, Pop would never settle in to his gospel music unless there was a beer or a shot of booze near by.

I suppose that was what he needed in order

to set the mood right for him to dwell, for a time, in the glow of God's Holy Love. Or maybe it was what he needed to generate the nerve that he lacked sober, in order to approach God after all the unholy things that he had done to me. Nevertheless this mood that he was now in, afforded me an escape without too much notice.

Every Sunday morning, from time to time, I even thought that maybe God was on my side after all. Any escape without injury was in my view a heavenly blessing. Blessed this morning, but when he gospel music has run its course and the mood had turned. What was for a moment, heavenly, would turn into my hell on Earth.

By evening when, upon my return, I knew that he would be calling me a motherfucker again. For now though, he sang along to the songs, "The Old Rugged Cross" and his favorite, "His Eye Is on The Sparrow." I would never forget that old gospel tune, and how it would give me the courage to perform the most dreaded task in my life. No, I would never forget, "His Eye Is on The Sparrow'. No one else on that fateful day in our futures would ever forget the song either. Little did I know that on that morning I would meet three people that would change my life forever.

As I did almost every Sunday morning I proceeded to knock on the doors of Mr. Miller for whom I purchased coffee and the Sunday news, Ms. Gloria and Mr. Harry, I always shopped for them on Sunday and got the newspaper. Ms.

Pearl always got the Sunday paper and some BC headache powder and the Catholic news from across the street at All Saints Catholic Church. All Saints was a large church, gothic in style. It took up an entire city block, running from 129th street and Madison Avenue to, 130th street and Madison Avenue. The church was also an elementary school, All Saints School, and it also housed the annex for Cathedral High School.

All Saints was a very racially balanced church. The student body was comprised of, Whites, Spanish and Negro's. The kid that stood outside of the church every Sunday was an odd acting and different looking guy whose mother still dressed him in knickers. His head was oversized for his body and though he was my age he had a five o'clock shadow from the full beard that grew on that youthful face of his.

In the past I had noticed him as he came and went to and from church or school. He was like me, always by himself and often set upon by some of the guys who lived in my block. I never intervened when in the past I saw him being assaulted by them.

For some strange reason, on this morning when I saw some of the guys throwing cans and bottles at him, I choose to step in and defend him. At that moment I did not entertain the thought that my own safety was in jeopardy. What I remember was that I did not want to see him demeaned and harassed by these other children who had also treated me in the same manner simply because I was different also.

The difference between him and I was that I stood up for myself and fought back. They soon came to the realization that even though my hands were always filled with books, it did not mean that I was unaware of the power and convincing methods a clinched and trained fist could effect when wanting to get your point across. I never ran from them. And even though they did not like me, none were any longer willing to test my resolve with acts of violence or threats.

Today they were not going to make this kid run, I remember thinking to myself. I was not, that day, going to permit it to happen. That day he needed me and I was in need, I was later to find out, in need of him. They had forced him off of the sidewalk in front of the church and into the gutter. They were throwing cans at him and breaking soda bottles at his feet as he danced around trying to avoid contact and broken flying glass.

I walked over to Butch, he was the ringleader, and told him to stop bothering my friend. Why I called him my friend I don't, to this day, know. But, that's what I said and my intent was to defend him. Even if it meant that I would sustain injury of some kind. I intended to defend him. And Butch saw that reflected in my demeanor and in the stare that I gave him and the other guys. He resorted to name-calling. "You piss the bed anyway." He said. "And you always smell like pee."

They all began to laugh and prance about in a gay and victorious manner. I responded with, "I pee the bed so that your nasty mother won't crawl into bed with me." Butch stopped laughing and resorted, "Don't talk about my mother." "I'll kick your ass if you talk about my mother." "Why?" I asked. "Was I not permitted to talk about your mother?" "Everybody else does." Butch became more angered and for the sake of pride and honor he pretended to advance toward me in a half attempt at provoking me into a fight. His boys stopped him. Ronald, one of the group said, c'mon man if you fight him you'll smell like piss for the rest of the week. They all laughed as they retreated, hurling insults as they removed themselves from the front of the church.

"My name's Peter, Peter Gutloff." "And you are?" "My name is Bobby." I replied. "Bobby Dickerson." Peter Gutloff, I thought, strange name for such a strange kid. He asked, "Did you really mean that you are my friend?" "Sure I am," "For the rest of our lives." I said, "Friends for the rest of our lives." The truth of that statement would not emerge to its fullest until January 23, 1970. When for the first time in my life I grew to realize how cold the snows that had fallen on the streets of New York that January could really be. On that day I found out that I had lost the only meaningful thing in my life. My friend was dead but that's a story for another time.

I told Gut, that's what I decided to call my new and only friend, that I had some things to do and that he was welcome to hang around with me until they were complete. When I was finished, I told him, we could go to 125th street and I would buy some pizza. Gut replied, "Yo Bob!" Gut said that Yo meant sure, ok, and hello. Depending on how you used it. Yo, Bob! What a pleasurable sound it became. Gut never got to know that Yo Bob didn't just mean sure, ok, and hello. To me, hearing him say it in his own special way always meant peace. Sometimes even now somewhere in between awake and being asleep, there in the shadows, I hear, "Yo Bob!" For a Moment or two in time I find peace again.

Peace in a place where the sun is always high, but never searing, and people smile not because they have just concocted a way to do something vile to you and get away with it. They smile just because they saw you. A place where, in the wonder of it all, peace becomes a refreshing stream, that flows from the tops of the mountains.

The water is sweet, cool, and never cold to the taste. A drop refreshes you and hydrates you to the fullest with pure normal natural human affection. Yes, sometimes there in the in-between I hear "Yo Bob!" And I remember peace. But I was running late and we set off about my business talking as we went, about stuff and things, about everything and nothing, about everybody and nobody.

Everything that was spoken between us was

the truth. Both of us knew then that we were always going to be truthful with each other. We knew that we would never argue because we could talk about anything. We also knew that we could never hurt one another. Since both of us had known so much pain. We knew that we were friends.

"Do I smell like pee to you?" I asked Gut as we walked toward 125th street and the pizza shop on the corner of Park Avenue. Gut answered, "Yo!" "Do I walk funny?" He asked. "Yes you do." I said. "And you dress funny too, but that's alright with me if it's alright with you." I added. "Yo!" He said and smiling broadly continued. "That makes us best friends right?" "Yo Gut!" I replied. At that Moment I felt so touched and humbled by the emotions I was feeling. This morning, I thought, I was the only one in my world. And now, now I have a friend.

So this is what friends do, I wondered. I'd never had a friend before and did not want to mess this up. Was I talking too much? I thought. Or maybe I am asking too many questions. What I did take notice of was how Gut was constantly looking at my bruises and cuts. Whenever I caught him he would divert his eyes and they would be welled up with tears, and he didn't say anything. I on the other hand wanted to break down and bring to an end this concealment of a horrible truth.

I wanted to confess to my new friend. What I wanted to tell him was how upon my entering a store or a room, everyone would pinch their noses together and express disdain for my presence. Some, while holding their noses, would wave their other hand in front of their faces. Those who did not know me were not used to my smell. People who knew me just dealt with me at arms length. It would be nice to share with him that my throat is raw and burns when I swallow because yesterday my father choked me until I almost blacked out. Not many people outside of those living in my neighborhood knew my secret.

Gut opens the door to the pizza shop and holds it for me as I enter first. That morning had brought me a bounty of eight dollars and seventy-five cents. We go up to the counter and order two slices each and an orange aide. Gut and I take our pizzas to a rear table beside the window. It was my choice so that my odor would not offend anyone.

Gut gobbles down his pizza so fast that I find it hard to believe that he hardly has a chance to taste it. Still chewing a mouthful of pizza Gut roars out, "One-more-time!" He orders two more slices and gobbles them down before I was able to take a bite out of my second slice. "Hit me, my good man," "One-more-time!" He roars again.

The name Gut sure fit him. It seemed as though he had a bottomless pit. After four one-more-times, and eight slices of pizza and five orange aides, we walked out into the crowd and sunlight of the afternoon of the day.

Across the street from the pizza shop, under the train trestle on Park Avenue was a hot dog stand. Hot dogs were ten cents. Gut said, "Let's get some hot dogs." So I said, "Yo!" I watched as he inhaled four hot dogs using only two bites each to consume each one. Gut did not pretend to enjoy eating. He left you with a vivid and lasting picture of his pleasure for food, even moaning and sighing in a hypnotic rhythm. Always engrossed in the absolute savoring of every bite or sip of what he was eating or drinking. What I learned about him that day was that while eating there was little if any meaningful conversation from Gut.

A master he was at enhancing the sale ability of a food item. If you saw him eating worms, the enjoyment that he showed while eating them would make you want to buy and eat a pound of them, and indulge, by the hand full the squirmy little creatures. There was no food made by man that I knew of, that Gut did not openly and shamelessly show great delight in its consumption.

I enjoyed being in and sharing his space with him. It was decided that we would walk up 125th street all the way to Eighth Avenue. And then we were going to Gut's apartment so that I could meet his mother and his sister, and we could listen to some records. As we walked, Gut decided that he would enjoy a Carvel ice cream cone, hot Spanish Peanut's from Woolworth's and a hamburger with mustard and that wonderful red pickle relish only served at Chock Full of Nuts. Then we headed to Gut's house.

It was getting close to dinnertime and Gut said that his mother would be upset if he were to arrive late. "What will happen if you are late?" I asked. "Will you get a beating?" With saddened eyes he looked me up and down and asked, "Is that what your parents do to you when you are late?" I had opened the door and there was no closing it now. I was obligated to answer him truthfully. "No." They don't beat me for being late." I said in a lighthearted manner. Gut asked, "What do they beat you for, Bob?" "They beat just for being me Gut." "Just for being me, that's all." "They beat me all the time," "Just for being me."

A half smile emerged from beneath my mask of sorrow. As always I tried to pretend that I was able to deal with things and that I was really fine. Pretending with Gut didn't fly very well. Nor was I able to, as I would soon learn, pull the wool over his mother's eyes either. They knew pain and agony. They knew rejection when they saw it.

Gut lived on 128th street right off of Madison Avenue in an apartment building next to PS. 24 elementary school, the school that was attended by James Baldwin, the masterful Negro writer. The building was gray in color on the front with a large stoop with four steps leading to the entranceway. The interior hall was wide and dimly lit. A large marble fireplace sat cold and unused on the left wall as you entered, just before you got to the steel meshed designed enclosed elevator. The stairs were narrow and located next to the elevator.

We took the stairs one flight up and to the first apartment door on the landing next to the stairs. Before Gut can insert the key, the door swings open. "We know each other, don't we?" I was shocked at who I saw standing there in the doorway of my new friends apartment. From time-to-time when hunger would become unbearable, I would go to the rectory at All Saints Church and ask the lady there for something to eat. Sometimes she would give me a sandwich or a piece of cake. Sometimes, just a few slices of bread with jam or jelly on them. She always gave me something to eat.

Never in the past had she scolded me for not telling her the truth concerning my plight, or for never telling her who my parents were. Whenever I went there to ask for food she would insist that I come inside. We would go and sit at the kitchen table. She would light a cigarette and pour a cup of black coffee. "Sit down." She would say. We had been doing this for a little over two years, so I immediately obeyed. "When's the last time that you've had a bath and some clean clothes, boy?" "My pants got dirty playing football and we were playing in the street and I slipped and fell in some dog pee." I offered up.

For some reason I was never able to change my story. She would continue to look me over for a while. Taking a puff here and a sip of coffee there as she walked around my chair or stood directly behind me. She would stop intermittently to examine a bruise, cut, or a bump. After swallowing deeply, she would say, "If you are going to continue to play so rough, I suppose I am just going to make sure you get something to eat." "You should take off those clothes and let me wash that dog pee out of them." "Oh no," I tell her.

She doesn't know that I've worn these clothes and underwear for two weeks now. This was how my parents would humiliate me. The last time someone had helped me was very costly to me. The person had no idea what was really going on. What the person knew was that I was a kid who was troubled.

The person saw the daily results of my parent's beatings. When the person confronted my parents, expressing concern about what they saw, I broke down and cried and started to shake with fear. Not in any condition to form a meaningful, understandable sentence. I began to mumble and stumble over my words as I tried to explain to Mom and Pop that I had not, to this person, said anything. I began begging my father, "Please, Pop!" I whined, "Please not today." "Don't beat me, I didn't say anything." "Don't you understand I didn't say anything?" I cried. Pop assures me in front of this person that he was not gong to punish me. "You misunderstood my boy." "Didn't he tell you he got hurt playing football?" "Yes," the person responded. "Well, we don't have a problem do we?" Pop asked. "No we don't." The person replied and walked away. Mom and Pop's smiles turn into frowns of contempt.

"All he did was ask me if he could give me a clean tee shirt." I tried to explain. "You cock sucking, nasty, dirty, bitch ass motherfucker." "Why were you putting our business out there in the street," He growled. In a way, I was prepared for what was about to happen. His assurances in front of my, would be rescuer meant nothing. What I did, at that moment, was give up all hope, including escaping my misery alive.

Even now, years later, I don't remember how long I was beaten that day. It seemed as though it lasted forever. I was happy when after awhile Peter's mother would no longer press the issue. "We do know each other, don't we?" She asked again. I wanted to run away or have the floor fall out from under me. But I couldn't move. Yes, ma'am I finally replied. "My name is Francis Boviair Gutloff. And Peter is my only son." "You will refer to me as Mrs. Gutloff." "Now what might your name be?"

"If you young sir, will excuse my boldness?" "I am in the habit of not allowing entry into my home by strangers." "Only friends cross this door sill." "Am I making myself clean or speaking at too rapid a pace for you to follow along?" "No ma'am," "Bobby ma'am," "yes ma'am," rolls out of my mouth as though I had lost all will of my own, taking a puff from the cigarette that she held between the first two fingers of her right hand, and before blowing out the smoke. She said "Bobby, nice name." "Peter," she said, (She pronounced his name Pee-Ta), "Ask your friend to come in and have dinner with us."

Mrs. Gutloff takes my chin in her hand and lifts my head backwards. I was afraid for her to look into my eyes for fear that they would expose all the secrets I held within. Tears of gratitude rolled down my cheeks. And I shrunk into a vat of emotion. Her voice soft and tender re-extends the invitation to me. I take a deep breath and with no further hesitation I entered the apartment. A new beginning I hoped, a new world.

Mrs. Gutloff called me Gut's friend. I'd never in my entire life been referred to as someone's friend. For the Moment I was happy and content. Even when we walked past the open bathroom door, I had no thought what so ever, as I gazed briefly at the medicine cabinet, of the mirror and the razor. I was, for the moment, safe and free. Time and experience has taught me that there is nothing anyone can do. Soon I knew the pleasures of peace would soon give way to the pains of reality, my constant Hell. For the moment I was engulfed in affection. I wasn't being hit I was softy touched. Rather than being yelled at I was being spoken to. Rather than being pushed aside, here in my new world, I was being embraced, tenderly.

Even though Gut and Mrs. Gutloff, seem happy, they, at the same time seemed to be worried. They seemed concerned with the extent of my injuries. She was so touched by the sight of me. Mrs. Gutloff kneels down and wraps her arms around me. The soft sweet smell of her perfume I have never forgotten. Still in the emptiness of the night I can still remember and smell the perfume in her hair. Most of all I remember the embrace that ended abruptly when she turned away so that I could not see her cry.

Once her composure was regained she said, "When you want to be cleaned up boy just let me know and it will be our secret." "OK." "OK Mrs. Gutloff," I said sheepishly. "OK" "When you're ready and not before Bob, not before you're ready." "No-one is going to hurt you here." "Not here, I promise." "Believe me and believe in me," she said. "Just trust with all of your heart and together we'll find a way out; together." "You're not alone anymore." "We'll always be here for you." "What you don't understand Bob, is that we will never do anything to hurt you. "No-one can hurt you when you're with us." "Who-ever they are." "They don't know who we are, or where we live, you're safe." "Do you understand?"

What I understood was that I was going to have to return to hell. That's what I told myself. They're going to beat me again I knew they were, as soon as I got back home. "They know," I tell myself. I'm so ashamed. They know the truth I feel my stomach start to curl and bubble. I want to go to the bathroom. Not to seek out the mirror and the razor, but to throw up. They know that I am innocent and how badly I want them to know that I am not beaten because I am a bad boy and all I want so much is to be liked, to be loved, I want to be human.

I was saved from pouring out my soul by a knock at the door. Gut said that it must be Jane his sister. She had forgotten her key. I was expecting to see a girl that looked like Gut. Instead, there walking into the room was one of the most lovely, shapely girls I have ever seen. "Hi!" "I'm Jane." "Are you staying for dinner?" She had on a tee shirt and blue tights and was wearing white tennis shoes and crew socks. I'll never forget how Jane looked when first I saw her. Jane looked sexy, but without the intention of looking that way. She dressed like that simply because that is how she felt comfortable. Nor did she exude to the fact that here I was, dirty and smelling bad, sitting in her mother's house.

All Jane was, was lovely and pleasant. "I've watched you play stickball on 129th street, you're very good." "But you really shouldn't take so many risks out there. "You know, diving for the ball the way that you do." "You could hurt yourself, you know?" "Is that how you hurt your eye?" She asked. Impressed is what I was that a girl so beautiful would pay any attention to me at all. Ashamed, because I didn't know how to explain to her that I played hard and took risk just to be accepted.

I never was, but at least everyone knew that

I was good, and the minor injuries that I sustained in the process of seeking acceptance, was, as far as I was concerned, well worth the pain. No one understood that nothing was less enduring than the pain I had to be subjected to on a daily basis. Jane's beauty and calmness caused my emotions to strain my whole body while trying to hear her every spoken word.

She takes a deep breath and say's, "Bobby you're so cute and sweet." "I could just hug you." "Please don't!" I screamed form within. "I could just eat you up." She moaned. I was melting from the inside, outward. I glowed in the wonderful and long desired encounter. Wow! Was the word that pierced my being at that moment, not only had I found a friend but I had also found my future. Mrs. Gutloff, Peter, Jane and I are going to be a family.

What, I thought, could be more wonderful, than to be a part of this family? My bubble burst and reality sank back to its normal resting place in the fore of my mind and I came back to earth. This time I landed uninjured, leaving no bumps or bruises. This time, I because of normal human expressions, landed on my feet. Of course, no matter what my child's mind assumed during a moment of rare fantasy. What was going to happen was that the four of us were always and forever going to be a family.

Mrs. Gutloff sat everyone at the small kitchen table. She served roasted chicken, green peas and rice and gravy. At first I was confused as to why there were two chickens on the table. Jane dissected and carved one chicken and served her mother, herself and me. It was then, as Gut tore away an entire leg at the thigh joint that I realized. The other chicken was just for Gut. I fidgeted in my chair not because of any discomfort that I was feeling. It was the sense of comfort that made me un-easy. To myself I thought, all of this is just a fantasy, when I blink, it's all going to disappear.

Turning to Gut, his face is covered with sweat and he is leaning forward over his plate. Mrs. Gutloff warns, "Pee-ta," "My God!" "Don't eat so fast." Gut smiles and yanks away the entire breast section and proceeds to gobble it down. "Pee-ta," "Pee-ta," Mrs. Gutloff sighs, "Mother," whines Gut in mocking response. "You're not eating Bobby," Jane laments. "Oh!" I say, lost in thought and the question catching me off guard. "I'm not very hungry," I say, as I pick and dig at my food with the fork. The food was very tasteful. What I had no taste for was the fact that before the streetlights came on; I had best have my butt in the house.

The sun was now out of the kitchen window. The reflection from the rays of the setting sun seared my eyes. I turn away from them as a single tear rolls down my cheek. Jane reaches over and with the gentleness of Christ she touches my elbow. My hand shakes. Gut puts his hand on my shoulder and sniffles. I tried not to openly expose the emotions that now raged within me.

What I released was a torrent of tears and sobs that flowed out of me against all the control I tried to expend. Here I was thinking I had saved Gut, when in fact he, his mother and sister were saving me. I put a fork of food into my thick mucus filled mouth knowing that its true flavor was being distorted by the taste of what the night would feed me fear and pain. Being painfully moved by my show of emotions that surfaced in me, Jane moved closer and hugged me tightly to her and said, "We will never leave you alone again." "Peter's your friend and the two of you are going to grow up and grow old as friends forever." "The two of you Bobby," "The two of you must always take care of each other," she said.

Through the tears of the moment I knew, it would be forever. For sure, at the time the world was at peace. Little did I know that forever would come in the form of a place called Viet Nam. For now, however, forever was always and a day. Jane hugs me tighter, smiles and says. "You have nothing to worry about." "No Bobby, honest, no-one will hurt you here." The comfort made me weak and I broke away from her embrace and his touch and decided that this was the right time to thank them and depart. One day, I thought, one day I will tell them the truth about my life and the unstable conditions that I lived in every day.

One day, I thought, but not today. The promise of peace has been there before but has always eluded me. One day, I thought but not today. Mrs. Gutloff and Jane hugged me and told me that I would always be welcome. Gut and I walked out of the apartment and down the one fight of stairs no words were exchanged. You could have cut the silence with a knife.

When we had exited the building Gut and I paused on the stoop. Looking up Gut said, "There's going to be a beautiful sky tonight." "What," I asked. "There's going to be a beautiful sky tonight," he repeated. "On clear and beautiful nights like this God can see everything and he protects all the innocent children." "You are innocent aren't you Bob?" He said. "Innocent." I asked. "Yo!" "Innocent," was his response. "Be innocent and God will protect you." "He sent you to protect me, didn't he?" After saying that Gut took me by the hand and said, "I'll walk you half way home." Hand and hand we walked up 128th street and on to Madison Avenue heading toward 129th street.

Am I innocent enough to warrant God's protection? I thought as I turned on to my block. At that moment the streetlights came on. Doomed, I said to myself as I broke into a run. It seemed as though the faster I ran, the further away my building got.

Pissy-issy! The girls jumping double-dutch taunted as I ran past them. Some of the guys from the block were choosing up sides for a game of steal the bacon. And the big guys, Freddie, Brother, Clyde, and Melton were playing cards on Freddie's stoop and sharing a bottle of beer.

As I jumped up on to the building stoop, I almost knocked Mrs. Margaret out of the way. "Bobby!" She said, "Bobby!" "He's not home slow down." "He's not home?" I asked. "No he's not home." She said. "Annie, Annie." Mrs. Margaret called through the open apartment window, which was to the left and level with stoop as you entered the building. Mom came to the window.

Before she could say anything Mrs. Margaret said. "Bobby is going with me to the fish market." "So don't worry about where he is, alright!" Mom said all right and ducked back into the window. It seems as though God could see me and my innocence after all. I looked up and the stars were bright in the clear sky and Mrs. Margaret loomed there against it like a brown angel all-aglow in the brightness of the streetlight. And I felt warm and safe as we proceeded to walk down the street.

The guy's playing steal the bacon moved out of the way. All of them greeted Mrs. Margaret. The big guy's scrambled to hide the beer bottle from her view, and the girls responded to Mrs. Margaret's command to fix their dresses that they had pulled back between their legs to prevent them from becoming entangled in to the rope as they jumped. "Fix your hair." "What's that on your dress?" "Pull up those socks and tell your mother that I said for to wash those tennis shoes." 'Pissy-Issy', I thought, as Mrs. Margaret shouted orders and gave commands. I might be Pissy-Issy, but I am walking with the Queen. No one usurped the authority of the Queen or questioned her power, and I was the Queen's favored subject.

As such, the benefits that came with her power, was now mine. I was ugly, I smelled bad, the only thing that I had going for me was the fact that I was a genius. And what good is it being a genius when brute force ruled the world? Pop ruled me with brute force. The evidence of that was apparent all over my body, and was evident by my fragile mental state.

Emotional instability was to become a condition from which I have never been able to escape from. My mind was ripped, torn and tormented by things that were beyond my understanding. Mrs. Margaret and I walked to the corner of 129th street and Madison. Turned left and continued on to Mr. Tony's Fish Market. "Vivian wants some fried Porgies for dinner." She said "How about you?" "Had dinner yet?" "Yes," "I had dinner with a friend." I replied, "Roasted Chicken, it was good too!" I said grinning from ear to ear. "You have such a lovely smile Bobby wish that I could see it more often." "It's very nice."

She then stopped abruptly and took my face into her hands she raised my face upwards so that our eyes met, "That world that you've been living in for so long by yourself." It must be so lonely in there by your self." "I can't, nor am I going to try to understand what you're going through." "Just remember what I am telling you, remember, even when I am dead and gone." "Always be just and fair." "Help who you can," "when you can." "And no-matter what may happen to you in you life," "Never hate Bobby." "Hate never builds up, it only destroys."

She then stood erect, patted my face bent over and kissed my forehead. I took what she said and stored her word's deep within my heart. That way they would stay with me forever, and I would never forget them. The emotion that most know as hate has always eluded me. I had never felt it before. And in all of my childish innocence, found that it was an unnecessary emotion. What sense did it make to dwell on a wrong committed against me by another who was just as imperfect as I?

I made it a point to commit myself to ponder deeply over the matter once I had gotten into bed. That way, I thought, I could stay awake and not wet the bed. And avoid a beating in the morning. We walked into Mr. Tony's. He greeted us. "Good evening Ms. Beckford." "What can I do for you?" "How are you doing Little Red?" That's the nickname that he gave me based on the reddish hew of my complexion. "Hi Mr. Tony," I responded. "You can sell me some fish that's not six weeks old." Mrs. Margaret said mockingly. "Oh!" "Mrs. Beckford, trust me. "This fish is only three weeks old if it's a day." Mr. Tony said smiling.

Mrs. Margaret smiled and asked, "How's the Porgies?" "The fish is fresh as of today; I got them in this morning, Mrs. Beckford." Mr. Tony proudly replied. "How many do you need?" The Porgies, Butterfish and Virginia Spots were laid neatly on beds of crushed ice. The floors were covered in sawdust and the fish was always fresh. Mr. Tony had taught me that if the eyes were dull and fish smelled fishy, don't buy the fish.

From time to time I did odd jobs for him, swept the floor, put out the cans of fish waste for pick-up, jobs like that. I enjoyed working for him and listening to his stories about Italy. Where he was born and raised up until he was twelve years old. And I loved being taught the fish business. Mrs. Margaret liked him too. They got great pleasure out of teasing each other. Here too was a place that I would often escape. A place of comfort rather than the mirror and razor in the dim confines of a bathroom, in the rear of a cold water rail road flat, in east Harlem.

Mrs. Margaret purchased six Porgies, head on and split up the middle. We exchanged good nights and walked out into the night. Darkness came early that time of the year. The streetlights set the avenue ablaze in a soft glow. The junkies were nodding out. Some so doped up that they nodded almost all the way down to the ground before springing back upright as though they had been shocked awake. The Wine-O's moved about in a perpetual stupor.

The neighbor's were picking up their milk crates and going into their apartments after spending the day monitoring the comings and goings of the residents and passersby, moving in and about on the block. It was a normal sight there on the block, older women sitting and ruling with an iron hand from their wooden thrones set up there on their front stoops.

With the setting of the sun, a cool breeze would fall upon the neighborhood, as was normal in the autumn time of the year, brisk, not cold. The chill in some ways was soothing to ones inner soul, a lullaby to the heat of summer, a prelude to the awaking of the coldness of winter.

In some ways, the death of what was, and the preparation for the birth of all things that were to come. All things and conditions, it seemed changed, except for my situations and my condition. It seemed only to grow graver. Mrs. Margaret and I talked as we walked toward our building. I told her that I was looking forward to seeing Gut the next day. We talked about how I was going to teach him how to play basketball and stickball and football.

"He's my only friend," I told her. "We're going to be friends forever." "You believe that don't you Bobby?" She asked. "Yes" I said, 'with all of my heart I believe it." "Then nurture that friendship and feed it with naught but love and devotion." "Let it grow and blossom into something grand and wonderful." "Give it time." "Sometimes you care more than you should."

"Don't let your willingness to love break your heart." "Bobby, forever sometimes only lasts until tomorrow," she said so very soft and lovingly. For my part I didn't really understand then what she meant in making such a profound statement. I was a genius, but none-the-less a child. Little did I know then that I would become a giver of my all to all, even when my all was not enough, and I had little of nothing to give.

A hero more destined to fail and to fall than to rise to success, happy, simplicity with no delusions of grandeur. Ralph Waldo Emerson once wrote, "Do not follow where the path may lead." Go instead where there is no path and leave a trail." I was going down a path not followed by most. Where it would take me, I for the most part, was going to end up in a place, a place that I will call, maybe tomorrow. Tomorrow, I have learned is inevitable, you or I being there is not.

When we arrived at our apartment building I noticed my brother Delroy sitting in the window. He was smiling a sly kind of smile, a smile that leads me to believe that he had knowledge of something that I did not.

I spoke to him. "Hi, Del.," I said. He did not answer. He just kept smiling that sly smile. "Don't forget my paper in the morning Bobby," Mrs. Margaret called out to me. "Alright I'll be there," I called back as she started to walk up the stairs to the second floor where her apartment was located, apartment 2R at the top of the landing.

Delroy opened the door before I had a chance to knock. Still smiling, he opened it as wide as it could be opened.

My heart stopped in mid-beat. Pop was sitting in the armchair. He had been drinking. "Who in the fuck told you to go running around in the street?" "When I told you to have your ass in this house before the street lights came on." "You think you're more fucking man than me or something?" 'You must smell your own piss or something," He said, spit flying from his mouth with each spoken word.

"I was with Mrs. Margaret Pop, Mom said that it was alright for me to walk her to the store," I said in a pleading sort of way hoping to escape his rage that was now reaching its peak. "Your mother didn't tell you shit you little cock-sucker." "I don't give a fuck who the hell you were with." "How many times do I have to tell you, I fucked for you, Mrs. Margaret didn't," He screamed. I tried to back out of the door, but Delory slammed it shut. Pop flew at me and punched me in the center of my chest. I fell backwards, held erect as my back struck the now closed door, he kicked me in the groin and I doubled over from the pain and fell to the floor.

He then began beating me with a razor strap. It tore into me ripping away old scabs that covered the result of pervious beatings. It opened old wounds. When he wasn't beating me with the razor strap he would kick and stomp me. He tried, while kicking me, to maintain his balance. But because he was in a drunken state he fell to the floor. While laying there he kicked out at me with all of his might, the kicks landing on the right side of my head, and the left side just above the ear. A sharp pain erupted in my head. I tried to crawl away but became engulfed in darkness.

My world turned black. I regained consciousness, after I don't know how long. I could taste the copper taste of blood in my mouth and feel the warm sensation of it flowing from my nose. It took me a while to realize where I was, or what was happening. There I was sitting with my back propped against the door. Blood was everywhere. Through blurred vision I saw Delroy. He asked, "Are you going to die now?" Mom cried out, "Leroy you killed him, he's going to die?" She fell to her knees and tried to stop the flow of blood. Her words and actions had no emotional effect on me. She had gone through the same ritual many times over the years.

I was frightened as I saw the deep red blood flow down onto the floor. The pain in my right side was unbearable. I tried to talk but was too weak. I wanted to keep my head erect but each time I attempted to do so it just slumped forward. I returned to the neither world of darkness. When I came to again I heard Pop ranting, "The hard head little punk made me do it, I'm not going to jail for killing his nasty ass!" "Delroy," he called out. "Help me drag this shit to the back stairs." "Mom asked, "For what Leroy?" "Stupid bitch" he resorted. "If they ask how he died we can say that he must have fallen down the backyard steps." "Don't be stupid Mom" replied. "We have to call an ambulance."

Pop ran from the house to find a phone. The pain was intense. Mom leaned over me and asked, "Can you hear me boy?" "Can you hear me, you filthy, dirty, nasty, little bastard, why can't you just do what the hell you're told to do?" "Why do you always have to create problems for us?" "You had better say that you got hurt playing football on the pavement just like before." You tell them anything else and you'll destroy this family." "You hear me," she screamed. I drifted off back into blackness. Somehow I felt a curious sense of relief. I thought to myself, "I'm dying." In my heart I thought it was over. This life of pain, agony and torment and living like an animal had come to an end. Pop beating me to death had set me free.

I saw through blurred vision faces spinning and distorted, the only things that appeared clear where the smiles on their face's. And their eye's looking at me with no emotion. If any of those blurred face's felt any compassion for me or felt any remorse. They did not reflect so in their eyes or smile's. The face's belonged to my two sisters and my brother. Delroy said very calmly and without an emotion, "Pop said that he killed him." "Yep Bobby's going to die."

My sister Edith chimed in, "Well he won't pee in bed anymore, right?" Delroy answered, "Right stupid, dead people can't pee. "No." "Dead people can't pee at all." "They can't breathe either." He leaned over me placing his ear to my nose. I took a deep breath. It was painful. Delroy stood up. "He's not dead yet, he's still breathing." Delroy said very matter-of-factly. "Since he knows everything, I wonder if he knows what dead is like." "And we get to see him die." Edith said. Delroy turned to her and said, "I hope that it's soon." "As he dies I'm going to yell in his ear." "What's it like?" They all laughed.

With every breath that I took pain ripped through my stomach, groin, and head. Blood continued to seep from my nose and mouth. I was relegated to taking short choppy breaths through my mouth. Breathing in that manner, I discovered, lessened the pain. As was the norm I suffered alone. There wasn't anyone who really cared. My greatest fear was being realized. I was going to die without ever knowing or having been loved.

What I remembered was the promise that I had made to myself. I was not going to give them the pleasure of seeing me beaten and defeated, I was not going to give in to self-pity nor did I expect to receive any from any member of my family. I wasn't going to lie down and die. I struggled to me feet. The pain was great but I was determined to make my way outside.

My protector, Mrs. Margaret, had not heard the commotion. And I felt that God was a phony and did not pay attention to the cries of little children. I realized as I tried to stand the pain only became more intense in my stomach. From a kneeling position I was able to open the door and crawl out into the hallway. I felt like I wanted to faint from the throbbing pain that raced through my head. What little strength I had left was ebbing away.

I was determined to make it outside even if I died in the process. I crawled a few feet and rested, crawled a few more and rested. The short distance of eight feet seemed like a mile. Upon reaching the outside, I crawled, head first down the steps. A crowd was gathering. As my head landed on the sidewalk below the stoop I heard someone say that the cops and an ambulance was coming. I vaguely remember hearing the sirens and seeing the flashing red lights.

As I rolled over onto my back I saw Pop's face looming above me. There was no concern in his face. His voice lacked compassion as he asked, "You trying to die?" "What are you doing out here?" "Out of the way," the ambulance attendant commanded, "Out of the way!" Pop moved out of the way along with the crowd that had gathered. Pop was completely without emotion as he told the police how I had injured myself playing football on the pavement without equipment. "He's a problem, always has been." Pop told the police offices. "I'm on the job too," he said. "Here's my shield." "Hard head makes a soft ass." The police officer said laughing. "You ever thought about putting his ass in the youth house?" "Not until now." Pop said in response.

The ambulance attendant leaned over me and asked me what had caused my injuries. I, in a weak voice said, "Pop." "He's calling for his father." Someone in the crowd said. My head moving from side to side I said "No Pop, no Pop."
"The kid is in bad shape, real bad shape," the attendant said. "Let's load him up and get him to the hospital." As they placed me on the stretcher I heard Mrs. Margaret yelling at Pop. "What happened to Bobby?" "What have you done to him now?" "I didn't do shit to him." "He did it to himself, so mind your business." The attendant asked, "Who's riding with him?" "He's hurt bad and we need one of the parent's to sign for his treatment." "I'll meet you at the hospital." "After this shit I need a drink." Pop said to him.
I was loaded into the ambulance. Through the window I could see the faces of the crowd. Mrs. Margaret was standing at the rear of the ambulance. There were tears in her eyes as we pulled away. The attendant screamed above the noise of the siren. "This kid is not going to make it if we don't get there soon." "These injuries didn't happen while you were playing football son?" "Talk to me, come on son talk to me," the attendant begged. I didn't respond. I just lay there waiting to die. When the ambulance arrived at the hospital nurses and doctors ran to the rear of the ambulance and pulled out the stretcher.
"I'm Doctor Brown. We're going to take care

of you just hold on." "Can you be brave for me?" I nodded my head yes. "Doctor Brown this is not a playground accident." One of the nurses said. Then everything faded into black. What I next became aware of was a distant voice from beyond the blackness. "Yo," "Bob." "Yo," "Bob."

As the world came back into focus I saw Gut standing next to the head of the bed. He was smiling that great big broad smile of his and holding my hand, at the foot of my bed stood Mrs. Gutloff. "You're going to be alright Bob." "It's been three days," "but you're going to be alright." Mrs. Gutloff said in an emotion-heightened voice. I tried to respond but realized that there was a tube running through my nose.

My mouth felt as though someone had filled it with sawdust. My body was ravished from head to toe in dull throbbing pain. I could feel the tube in my throat and the I.V. needles in both of my arms. I felt Gut's hand tightly clasped in mine. With great effort I squeezed his hand as hard as I could. A tear in its warm and salty splendor rolled down my cheek and into my mouth. The tube attached to a bag hanging from the side of my bed lead to and was inserted into my penis.

Excited, Mrs. Gutloff reached for and pressed the call button for the nurse. I heard the sounds of running people converge on my bed. "What's wrong?" The nurse asked while pushing Gut out of her way. She franticly began checking my I.V. tubes and bottles. Then a look of amazement came over her face. "He's awake," she screamed. "Get the doctor he's awake." Regaining her composure she whispered, "My God, thank you, I've got to get the doctor." "He's awake." At a sprint the nurse's aide, a tall slender man, left the side of my bed to retrieve to the doctor.

In what seemed like mere seconds in time there were four doctors and a group of nurses were leaning over me checking every bodily function possible in a human being. I strained to see through the crowd of medical staff. What I wanted was to see Gut, my friend. "Follow my finger with your eyes." One doctor commanded. "Does this hurt?" Another asked while pressing and probing different parts of my body. "Do you know where you are?" "What's your name?"

The questions continued as well as the probing. Until a doctor stepped forward and asked, "Do you remember me?" "I'm Doctor Brown." Weakly I said "Doctor Brown." "Yes, Doctor Brown." He smiled and ordered everyone to go back to his or her normal duties. Doctor Brown sat down on the side of my bed. Then he turned to Gut and Mrs. Gutloff and asked them to leave and come back later. "No!" I called out. He smiled again and told them, "It looks like he wants the two of you to stay." "Am I right son?" I nodded my head up and down and said, "Yes." I reached out to Gut and he walked over and paced his hand in mine. "After what you're just been through I suppose it will be alright for them to stay." Doctor Brown said, "But just for a little while son." "They've been here day and night for three days." "You need to rest, you've been through quite an ordeal and so have your friends." He then stood up and I noticed how tall he was.

His skin was almost pure white and as smooth and flawless as the statue of David by Michelangelo. His hair was curly brown and his eyes were as blue as the oceans of my dreams and the kindness reflected in them melted the hardest of hearts. "I'll contact your parents." He said. "Maybe now they can come and visit you." "I'll be back in about an hour, so that you and I can talk, alright?' "Yes!" I said. And he walked away almost skipping. "Mrs. Gutloff. What did he mean maybe now they will come see me?" Mrs. Gutloff told me not to get upset. She said that Mrs. Beckford and her daughter came to visit but no one else.

A flood of tears flowed from my eyes. Deep uncontrollable sobs emerged from the deepest recesses of my being. And a hurt that I never experienced before grabbed and squeezed my heart, the feeling so painful that breathing was not without great effort. Every thing looked distorted because of the welling up of tears in my eyes. I was blinded by them as the emotions poured fourth from the floodgates of my heart. "Why!" I cried out. "Why what Bob?" Mrs. Gutloff asked. "Why don't they love me?" Calm down Bob, please calm down." She pleaded her voice choked and breaking. My breathing grew more labored. "Nurse, Nurse!" "My God nurse, get the doctor!" "Please." She screamed. "Get the doctor!" "Why don't they love me?" "Why don't they love me?" I said over and over again. I didn't want to utter those words aloud, but my heart just kept on screaming them.

In moments the nurse was by my side stroking my forehead, her hand moving upward and into my hair. "You've got to let go of his hand son." She commanded Gut. "I won't and I can't." Gut yelled back at her. "He's my friend." "Alright then baby, hold your friends hand." The next voice that I heard was Doctor Brown's. "Robert!" "Calm down this is not helping your condition any." "Nurse," he ordered. "Get the syringe for me." I didn't feel anything except a sensation of falling into a deep dark hole. Then all was once again engulfed in black. A dreamless state of nonexistence engulfed me, a pure deep black darkness. The last thing that I remember was the feeling of Gut's hand in mine. It was the feeling of real affection. It was peaceful.

When I came to again Doctor Brown was standing at the foot of the bed talking to a group of doctors and a well-dressed blonde woman in a brown business suit. I pretended to be asleep and listened to their conversation. Doctor Brown was explaining my medical condition. "This is Robert Dickerson." "He's eight years old and has suffered severe trauma to his head, chest, kidney's, spleen and liver." At present his condition is stable. "We will be transferring him off of intensive care today." "Because of his emotional state I am very worried." Doctor Brown said. "There are a number of old unexplained injuries all over his body along with open infected sores, one being on the foreskin of his penis." "There is also trauma caused by penetration to his anus." He continued.

The blonde woman in the business suit asked could any of my injuries be medically explained. "Rape explains the trauma to his anus." One doctor offered. "The sores and infections can be attributed to constant exposure to urine and lack of care, like laying in it all the time and going unwashed." "What about the other injuries?" She asked. "The parents said that he was playing tackle football on asphalt without protective equipment." Doctor Brown stated. Laughing another doctor asked. "Who was he playing with, the New York Giants?" "Well Mrs. Garrison, as the child welfare representative what do want to do?" Doctor Brown asked.

"Do we release him back to his parents?" "There is no doubt that this is one of the most horrible cases of child abuse that I have ever seen." "There is not a doubt in my mind that this child has been raped and beaten." "This is the worst case that I have ever seen, or, I believe any of you have ever seen here at this hospital or here on God's green earth." "The parents haven't been here to visit and seem to be completely disinterested, but are sticking to the football story." "I find something very disturbing about this picture." "We need to get to the bottom of this matter." "I'll just have to talk to Robert when he stops pretending that he's asleep." "Won't I Robert?"

It seemed that my pretending to be asleep act had not fooled Doctor Brown. I opened my eyes and looked at him, but was not going to confirm what I knew he already had concluded. I was an abused child. And I wasn't going to put my parents in a position where they would be arrested and jailed. If I did that, how would I ever win their love? Tears of panic streamed down my face as my brain raced and screamed at the thought of being taken away from my family. All of a sudden the burdensome chores and the beatings and relentless verbal abuse seemed not so bad after all.

The room became suddenly cold. I shook and trembled with fear and embarrassment, the fear of being placed in a home with strangers. Embarrassed because they knew what the fat man with the one large deformed eye had done to me. Now Mom and Pop were going to find out. I wanted to disappear into the never, never, world before Doctor Brown and the social worker Mrs. Garrison had a chance to ask me any questions. I was terrified because there was no saving me from the lies I knew had to be told. Mom had ordered me never to disclose anything concerning what was happening to me. If I did, she said, I would destroy the family.

Keeping the family secrets will invoke

stronger and more caring emotions towards me. I presumed. I decided to, for the first time in my life to willfully and openly lie, not only to Doctor Brown and Mrs. Garrison, but also to myself. I knew that from that point on, no matter what happened to me, the lie would make anything else that I could ever say unbelievable.

The fact that they already knew the truth did not matter. If what they suspected was not confirmed by me. I knew nothing would be done to my parents. And maybe, my childish mind conceived, maybe they'll even allow me to keep the tube in my penis, and I won't be able to pee in the bed anymore. Then Pop would have no reason to beat me.

"Hello Robert." "My name is Mrs. Garrison." "I'm from the Department of Welfare." "Do you know what that is?" I said, "Yes." "I want to help you, and so does Doctor Brown and these other doctors." "Will you help to us to help you by telling us what happened to you?" "Ok!" I said. "What is it that you want to know?" "We, all of us Robert, would like you to tell us what happened to you." "How did you end up here?"

"Well, what happened was I was told by my mother and father not to play tackle football at the playground without shoulder pads and a helmet." "But I did it anyway, and when I caught the football and was trying to make a touchdown the other guys all jumped on top of me and I got hurt and when I got home my father called the ambulance and I woke up here." I said in a rapid manner for fear that if I spoke slowly I would forget the lie. "And Robert do you know what an anus is." Mrs. Garrison asked. "Yes." "It's the hole in my butt and I can tell you how I hurt it too." I blurted out. "Tell us how Robert, we'd really like to know." One of the Doctors asked.

"I was climbing a fence one time and I slipped and one of the spikes went in my butt hole." "It hurt too." I smiled while telling that lie in hopes that the smile would put the lie over the top as more convincing. "And Robert what about your penis do you know what a penis is?" Doctor Brown asked. "It's my wee, wee." "It got caught in my zipper one time and I pee the bed too and I hide it from my Mom and Pop and the pee makes me itch and I scratch a lot and when I scratch a lot I bleed and"

"Stop, stop Robert!" Not one word of this is the truth. "It's all a lie." Mrs. Garrison screamed. "How can we help you if you lie to us?" "I'm not telling lies, I'm not." I yelled at the top of my lungs, faking tears in the attempt to be more believable. "You're not telling the truth." She yelled back. "Somebody did these things to you, who?" "Nobody did anything to me." "I hurt myself playing and wetting the bed." I cried. "Everybody loves me and nobody would hurt me." "Now leave me alone!" "Just leave me alone." I begged.

Inside I felt very bad because I had to lie. The look of disappointment on Doctor Brown's face made me cry for real. "Alright Robert we won't talk about those things anymore." Doctor Brown said softly. "Let's talk about school." "Do you go to school?" "I don't, well not to regular school anyway." "I got sent to a school for special children downtown." They have a room for me down there and different teachers come to teach me things. And once a week a doctor comes and asks me all kinds of questions, and they give me a lot of test." "My Pop said that I have to go there because I'm real smart and that white people just want to find out what makes me tick."

"Is that what your Pop says Robert?" "I've been listening very closely to how you present yourself." "You seem to be trying to appear more childish and immature than what you really are." "It's not a very convincing act," Mrs. Garrison Said. "Does your Pop beat you because you're different?" "Does he beat you because you're smarter than most children your age?" I told her that my Pop does not beat me all. "What I don't like, Mrs. Garrison, is how you play on words." "If you think for an instant that you are more intelligent than I am and that you can trick me into confessing something to you and these gentlemen that would prove your theory that I am an abused child, Mrs. Garrison, you do, I believe, give yourself more credit than you deserve." I resorted, forgetting to continue my pretence of childish innocence. She turned and smiled slyly at the doctor's and said, "Point proven." I knew then that the pretense of childish intellect was over. I had blown it. I had outsmarted myself.

"I think I have found out everything that I need to know Doctor's, this conversation is over as far as I am concerned." "Robert let me be frank with you, alright?" "I know all about you and your I.Q. and that think tank that you attend." You understand far more than what pretend not to."

"Understand this, you little smart ass." "The next time you come here it may very well be feet first and cold dead." "You get my meaning?" "The next time they will be tying a tag to that big toe of yours." She then pulled out a piece of paper and wrote on it. "Here's my home and office number." "Call me when you decide that the truth can protect you." She placed the paper in my hand and turned and walked away. Doctor Brown told me that they were going to keep me for three or four more days and then I could go home. "I'll contact your parents Robert to let them know that one of them will have to sign the release papers before you can go home."

With a look of rejection and disappointment on his face he walked away. The others followed. Doctor Brown suddenly turned to face me and said. "Robert I had a long conversation with Mrs. Beckford and her daughter." "I thought that there would be a certain degree of trust between us?" "You disappointed me." He knows the truth, I thought, but I wasn't going to change my story. I was going home to my family.

A male nurse's aide was approaching me with a stretcher accompanied by a young doctor whom I presumed to be a resident. The doctor said that he's going to remove the tube from my nose and from my penis and I was going to be transferred to another ward. The removal of both caused me momentary discomfort. It felt good to be free of them.

I was concerned that once the tube was removed from my penis that I would pee the bed when I got home. Would Pop beat me for it again? I dared not dwell on it. I thought only of going home and hoped that Gut would come soon to visit me. It was also strange that aunt Lolla had not assumed her rightful position by my bed plying me with food. Reality sank in. It was the normal treatment of me by my family. I still remained unworthy and unwanted. They never heard me when I told them that I loved them. The days moved forward quickly, day blending into faded shadow's of dusk into the blackness of night, night, into the soft glow of the dawn, then into the brilliant rays of the day.

Still Mom and Pop did not come to visit me, Gut came every day after school and brought me a hot dog with onions, mustard and sauerkraut. Mrs. Margaret and Vivian came, as did Uncle Book and Aunt Jessie. No one else, expect one of my instructors, Mr. Bongiovani. He was my German and American history instructor. The first time that I went into the bathroom I was able to see the results of the pounding that I took to my face.

One side was still swollen and almost black with bruises. I got to see me as others had been seeing for the past eleven days, a beaten and battered little boy. I understood then why there was so much concern, and Mrs. Garrison's words rang out as loud in my head as the bells in the tower of Big Ben. "The next time you come here it may very well be feet first and cold dead." What hope for some change in my life style were now crushed and torn, all the terrors that I, in my childish innocence envisioned, were about to become a reality. The happenstances of life are unavoidable. The minds of men are unchangeable. My plight was predictable.

So I walked out of the hospital heading for the inevitable. I knew nobody was going to come to pick me up. So I struck out into an uncertain future. One thing for certain, I was either going to be sent to the hospital feet first and cold dead, or cold dead and feet first. When I realized those two options, were my only options. The former, nor the latter, offered much in the way a future.

I was resolved at that moment to once and for all to endure all that was unendurable in my life. I will escape and create a future for myself that will be void of pain. Even hate will be absent, a faded memory never again brought to mind. In my childish innocence, as I have said, I thought these things and dreamed those dreams as I waked toward the one thing I feared most of all, home.

What I did know and understand was that the limits of my endurance had not only been reached, they had been exceeded. What I did know and understand was that what I was about to face must be faced. I had to survive at all cost. And with staunch determination and resolve, I would. There is no greater master of my fate, besides God other than myself. God it seemed had turned the greater burden over to me. No doubt I was alone. Little did I realize then that the adventure was just the beginning of a long and obstacle paved road that I was doomed to follow. If only then I would have known where it would take me.

The path that I embarked on that day would prove to be, for the rest of my life, paved with stones and obstacles. Rather then roses and spring flowers. I would have avoided taking such a path. For short distances I was able to evade the thorns and thistles, the hard and unforgiving stumbling blocks that would have caused me to fall. The height, width and breath of the obstacles did not allow me to go over or around them. I could only fight my way through them as they were encountered.

My quest to find the peace, I thought awaited me at the end of the path that I had chosen, compelled me to go through them. Leaving me weakened but still determined. The ill winds of life that sometimes blew me off course have but bent my integrity and morals at times. They did not diminished nor break my will to survive. Besides the offering up of these thoughts of a child, that transposed themselves into dreams yet to unfold that I have shared with you. Let me continue guiding you down the path where I tripped, stumbled and crawled.

From 135th street, my journeys have taken me either through or around the Abraham Lincoln projects. There on the grassy section were round signs that read, "Do not walk on grass." The playgrounds and children were clean and well cared for. The buildings were spotless. My choice was to evade as much human contact as possible. So rather than take the shortcut through the projects, I made the decision to walk around the outskirts of it, so down 135th street, toward Park Avenue I walked.

At Park Avenue, I turned right. Once I had passed the projects, across from the elevated railroad tracks that would bring the white people into the city from Connecticut and White Plains. They rode down from their ivory towers to work as lawyers and doctors in the ghettos. They owned all of the businesses up and down 125[Th] street. People of color were allowed to run their elevators and work out of their back rooms and factories, but could not live in their neighborhoods unless they were live in maids.

There were factories lining both sides of Park Avenue from 135th to 125th street and Park Avenue. Off to my left on 132nd street and Park Avenue, was the welfare building where from time to time I engaged in a football game during the winter months. There if not mindful, you, once tackled, would find yourself face down in dog droppings.

Upon this grassy lawn, the neighborhood residents would walk their dogs. Dog droppings and dreams of becoming Y.A. Tittle went hand and hand. Those of us who were lucky would stuff the shoulders of our shirts with either cardboard or towels to resemble the well equipped New York Giants. Our only helmets, for the most part was courage and determination. Green grass on which to play was rare in a concrete jungle.

As I passed 130th street on the corner of 129th street and Park Avenue, there was a Shell Gas Station. Where, more often than not, we would, while playing stick ball in the street, lose our ball to a home run on top of its roof, thus ending the game unless one was agile enough to climb up its side to retrieve it. Most of the time that game just simply ended, and I, most of the time, was the villain, because it was I that hit the home run.

Almost home, one half a block away from uncertainty. I was a moment away from life's reality. The building, numbered sixty, seemed to loom above all the others. Its small five-step stoop appeared more pronounced than the rest. The five-step walk-up felt like a mile of climbing. Fatigue set in and the approach to the front door drained me of what little strength I had possessed. It was dinnertime when I knocked on the door. Delroy answered, and opened it. He just stood there smiling that Delroy smile. The smile that said, "I know something that you don't."

"It's Bobby." He called out. "What the fuck is he doing coming up in here while we're eating dinner?" Pop responded. "What in the hell are you doing here?" Pop asked, "I was going to pick you up tomorrow." "You ain't learned shit boy, have you?" "What do you expect, dinner?" "No Pop." "It's alright I'm not hungry." "All I wanted to do was come home." Pop screamed, "You just come walking in here expecting dinner like you belong here." "Your mother did not cook enough for you, so you walk up in here demanding to be fed." "Not here, not now, not ever." "You son of a bitch, you should have died."

Delroy just stood there and smiled. And I, I was, after so long away, home. Nothing had changed. I had expected at the least to be fed. Instead I hungered more for love and affection and sympathy than I did for food. I, no doubt, had in fact, returned home to what had always been. Mom never looked up from her plate and my sisters sat eating and snickering. Delroy asked, "Do you still pee the bed?" I didn't respond so he walked over to where I was standing and kicked me in the shin. "Do you still pee the bed?" He asked more forcefully. My sisters snickered louder. "Starting shit already huh prick?" Pop bellowed. "No Pop." I sheepishly replied. Delroy asked if I still wet the bed, then he kicked me.

"Dad, see he just walked in here and he's already starting stuff." "Please Pop." I implored.

"Can I sit down?" "Sit where you stand motherfucker." He said. "I don't want your nasty ass on nothing that looks like my chairs." He jumped up from his chair and for an instant I thought that he was going to hit me. He stopped inches from my face and screamed, "Didn't I say sit, cocksucker?"

Without hesitation I flopped to the floor. Delory and my sisters taunted me by waving food in front of my face and I sat with my knees drawn up to my chin in the corner beside the door. My heart sank and the fear of the night and what would happen during the night overwhelmed me.

The morning next, I knew, would re-introduce me to the pain that for the past eleven days had been lacking. For an instant in time I just wanted to pee in my pants and get it over with. Why wait? The pain will be no greater in the morning than it would be right now. Instead of peeing in my pants I thought it best to figure out a way to get into the bathroom. Therein comfort awaited me. Waiting there for me was the medicine cabinet, my old friends, the mirror and the razor. After they had finished their meal, Pop ordered me to wash and dry the dishes. Mom still had not acknowledged my presence. When the chores were competed, Pop told me to go bed. There were no sheets and covers on it, just the faded brown rubber sheet. Never the less I lay down on it and drifted off to sleep.

It was a dark sleep, dreamless, and soundless. Only the chill wind that blew up the airshaft and through the window over my uncovered body reminded me throughout the night that life still existed outside of the blackness that engulfed me. The dark is where I was always able to hide. Therein I was invisible.

During the twilight periods, when I was neither asleep nor awake did I feel any sensation of discomfort. The discomfort was abject fear. The rush of cold air is what I felt every morning when Pop yanked away the covers to expose the wet and frightened little boy beneath them. Each time that I emerged from the deep sleep, being awakened by the embrace of the momentary rush of the cool wind, I expected to be rained on by random blows and curses.

When I became aware of my whereabouts it became apparent, and I understood for fractions of seconds, that I was asleep un-covered. And what I felt was simply the gentle touch of the wind. Sleep would once again become my safe port away from the storm and boiling sea of my life. Details of the morning are not at this point necessary to elaborate on. As was the norm I was wet and the beating just as brutal. My rounds were made. Newspapers were brought for my regular customers and coffee was purchased for Mr. Miller at Mr. Frank's candy store.

As each individual looked at me I saw different levels of concern and sadness in them, Mrs. Margaret cried. Mr. Frank reached out to touch my face from behind the counter but stopped just as his fingers felt the warmth of my bruises. As staunch as he was, tears welled up in his eyes. Rather than touch me he pulled his hand back and reached for a small brown paper bad and into he put five Davy Crockett cookies in it and handed them to me. Diverting his eyes from me he called out, "next," but there was no one else in the store to wait on. "Thanks Mr. Frank." I called out as I walked out the store.

"Bobby!" He called. Then his voice trailing off into almost a whine he said "Oh Bobby, Oh Bobby." He didn't say anymore, but the sound of concern in his voice told me what he wanted to say. The sight of me in the condition that I was in broke his heart. The only thing that I could do at the moment was offer up a smile and wave to comfort him. From the corner of my eye I noticed Mr. Frank turning up a small white Dixie cup to his lips, and it wasn't even Sunday. Mr. Irving, who owned the grocery store next to Mr. Franks, gave me two containers of milk, six good-o sodas and five pounds of potatoes and some sliced slab bacon and ten rum and butter toffee cadies.

Mr. Tony gave me some fish. Dr. Mills, who later on in my life played a major role in my escape from Pop and the others, owned the drug store on the corner of 129th and Madison, called me inside and gave me a bag that had cotton balls and first aid cream in it. Even the guys from the block didn't torment me that morning. They just lowered their heads and eyes and said, "Hi Bobby." They all knew what had happened.

They saw and understood the cycle of my life, for now, just for today, I was not the object of their taunting and disdain. For now, even to them, I was human. Oh how wonderful it was to walk freely among mankind without the torment that had become the norm being heaped upon me daily. In reality I knew deep down inside that they really, really didn't believe that when I was hurt, I cried, when I was cut, I bled and that blood was just as red as theirs.

When I would bite into a hot dog, or a hamburger, or a hero sandwich, I savored the flavors of each just as much as they did. I was human with desires and emotions just like they had. I decided that since things were going so well I would go to visit Gut. The day was crisp but not cold.

When I turned unto 128th street I heard my favorite two words. "Yo Bob!" Gut was running toward me in that off balanced manner that made you want to reach out and grab him to keep him from falling, his left arm bent at the elbow, and moving back and forth across his upper body.

His over sized feet and the way he walked caused his shoes to run over at the heels. The heels were almost non-existent except for the inner portion. The upper part of the heel of the shoe twisted out of shape, this distortion of his footwear caused his shoes to flap up and down on his feet as he walked.

Nevertheless, in all of his imperfections, his over sized head, his protruding overly round butt, slew footed and lacking the desire to change clothes or brush his teeth as often as he should. He was my friend, and a sight for the sore eyes. He was my friend, a welcomed sight for a torn soul. "Yo Gut." I called back a greeting that for the two of us would last for a lifetime, short though it turned out to be.

"What ya doing!" He exclaimed as he reached me. "Looking for you Gut," I professed happily. "Well, you found me." "What are we going to do?" He asked. "Walk and dwell among the living." "Eat, drink and savor the fruits of life." "Let's live life for today." I said as I reached for him to get a hug. "Let's go to the movies." "Okay, Bob." "Let's go Gut." I responded. "Do you always speak in quotes?" "You sound kind of crazy sometimes, ya know?" Gut asked. "I don't know." I said. "True nervous, very dreadfully nervous I had been and am, but why do you say that I am mad?" I said, Quoting Edger Allen Poe. "That's why?" Gut said laughingly. "Gut, you've got to understand one thing." The quotes are those of dead men. It really should be apparent to you by now that no-one ever really hears you until you are dead."

"Fuck me!" Gut blurted out. "That's heavy." "Deep too, just like whale shit." "Deep!" "I didn't know that you had such a dirty mouth." I told Gut. "My mouth is not dirty dear friend, I am just being expressive my dear friend, just being expressive." "What a wicked web we weave." "You quoted again Bob." "So I guess I can be expressive." "Two tears in a bucket don't fill it, mother fuck it." "Let's go to the movies." We roared with laughter as walked and half skipped toward Fifth Avenue on our way to 125th street.

With limited funds we had a choice of three theaters, The West End, the Harlem Opera House or the Regan. Neither could compare with the RKO or the Lowe's. The first three showed three movies and cartoons. But were dirty and showed only old movies. The RKO and Lowe's always had the newest releases. And admission was Fifty cents; the others were only a quarter. The Harlem Opera House was showing The Sands of Iwo Jima starring John Wayne, my hero, that's what we decided on. The Crawling Eye was also being shown, a war flick and a horror movie. What else could you ask for?

The days, weeks and mouths flew by. Nothing changed much in my life except for my closeness to Gut. We became more than brothers. We spent many an hour just in conversation about our deepest emotions. Our future desires. Gut wanted so badly to become a New Your City fireman. We spent countless hours at the fire station on Park Avenue between 128th and 127th streets. He knew everything there was to know about fire engines and hook and ladders. Whenever a fire engine was on its way to answer an alarm, Gut without warning would take off running behind it in that slow clumsy way of his, sometimes for blocks, until at last he would arrive, though late all of the time, and the fire out.

They treated him as somewhat of a human mascot, he and I were allowed to sit in the engine as the fireman loaded up the hoses and equipment. Gut was in heaven. There was this look on his face that was part frown, part smile, all pride. Gut called it his copping his grand face. I was happy because he found a place to belong, on the other hand. I didn't care at all for hook and ladders or fire engines. When teased by the guys in the block about following the crazy fuck around looking at fires. I simply said, "He's my friend." "When I am not standing beside him, I will run behind him wherever he may go, even in to hell." I really didn't believe that they ever understood.

The fact of the matter is that what they thought or understood never mattered. It was his dream, his joy, and I shared them with him. That's what mattered to me. There wasn't, nor would there ever exist a distance between us. Few were the waking hours when we were apart, odd in our own respects, happy together. Gut told me once, just out of the blue, "Bob." He said. "What we are, are brothers in arms." "We depend on each other."

To this day I don't know what prompted him to say such a thing. Nor at the time did I realize what profound a statement it was. Brothers in arms; He told me that when I was just 12 years old. There was no war. I had, however, considered the possibility of joining the Marines

Corps when I turned 18. The sight of a Marine did to me what a fireman did to Gut. A Marine awakened every fiber of my body, provoked me to walk beside them in step every time I would encounter one.

The crispness of the Tropical uniforms, the cut lines of their class "A" Greens and the Red, White, Blue and Gold of their Dress Blues were a sight that would drive me to march to the throngs of the Marine Corps hymn. I could almost hear the cadence being called by the slender and tall Drill Instructor. They looked like the ultimate warriors. I worshiped them as the grand protectors of the greatest nation on earth.

My first memory of a Marine was my uncle Adolphus. An oil painting of him in his Dress Blues hung over the piano in my grandparents house in Alberta Virginia. In detail, I can still remember him spit and polished in his class "A" Greens when he would come home on leave. The vivid memories that I, even today have of him bewilders my family. There was a fondness that he had for me that once led me to believe that he was my real father.

Uncle Adolphus took me everywhere with him. It was me that he favored most. We had the same complexion, the same red hair, and as the old folks would say, I looked like he spit me out. Odd though it may seem I have memories of him from the time that I was one year old. His death at age 21 left me devastated and I never got over it. He was involved in a car accident while serving in Hawaii.

When they sent his body home he was laid out in full Dress Blues a copper colored coffin with a glass shield that separated him from loving touches. When someone picked me up to look at him in repose, I don't remember, for the life of me, who. I began to beat on the glass screaming, "Wake up Uncle Adolphus, wake up."

What I did not realize, nor did I understand, as a three years old child, was that he was in a sleep of death, a sleep that he would never awaken from. As strange as it may seem, to you, the night that he died, my mother, Delroy and I were living in Richmond Virginia with my mother's sister Emily Lee and her two children. We all lived on Edgewood Avenue in a large house in the upstairs portion. It was a warm night.

I remember my mother and her sister Emily Lee walking around the house in their slips in order to be as cool as the hot humid night would allow. There was calm, and a stillness about the night that seemed to put them on edge as they prepared us for the bed, they, for some reason could not seem to get it together. Once all were at rest on the soundless dark night, I could hear them, my Mom and Aunt Emily Lee, tossing and turning in fits of unrest.

For some reason, I can't explain why, I was drawn to the window. To my joy there stood Uncle Adolphus looking up smiling and waving at me. It was not the type of wave one expected from another when saying hello. It was the kind of wave someone gives when waving goodbye. I waved back and ran from the room and sat at the top of the stairs waiting for my mother and aunt to open the door so that I could be the first to jump joyfully into his arms.

The doorbell rang. Once, twice, three times in succession. Aunt Emily Lee walked from the room and saw me sitting on the top step. "What are you doing out here Bobby?" she asked. She said, "It's two o' clock in the morning." "I wonder who that can be ringing the bell at this hour?" "Uncle Adolphus," I said, he's standing there at the door. "Annie, Annie!" Adolphus is home she yelled. Her frantic call drew Mom out of the bedroom, and to the top of the stairs. Aunt Emily Lee leaped down them two steps at a time.

She flung open the door and there was no one there. "There's nobody here Bobby," she said. "I hope you're not playing with the door bell." "Are you?" "Nope," I said. "It was Uncle Adolphus." "I saw him from the window and he waved at me." Mom chimed in. "It must be the kids playing games." "Bobby's just lying," "Adolphus is in Hawaii, get to bed boy." Mom ordered. We all went back to bed. Moments later, the bell rang. Once, twice, three times. Mom and Aunt Emily Lee went to the door again. Nobody was there.

They went to bed mumbling to each other that if it happened again they would call the police. Again the bell rang. Once, twice, three times. Angered they bolted from the room and down the stairs. Upon opening the door they found no one there. Aunt Emily Lee, having grown tired of what she assumed was a group of children at and about playing pranks on a hot humid night, called the police. In short order two of them arrived. "What seems to be the problem?" The taller officer asked, as the shorter officer checked the push button on the bell. "Some kids are playing with our bell officer." Mom replied. "It's driving us crazy." "Are you sure that you don't have a short on this thing?" The shorter of the two asked and then pressed the button and held it so that there was a continuous ring. He did this few a times.

"Doesn't stick," He said to the taller one. "Doesn't seem to be shorted out either?" He said questionably. "We'll check out the neighborhood ladies." The taller one said. "Try to get some sleep." At that moment the telephone rang. Aunt Emily Lee said, "I'll get the phone Annie." "You talk to the police." "Oh my God no." "Not him, no not my brother." Mom and the police ran into the living room where Aunt Emily Lee was screaming and flailing her arms in the air. I ran from the bedroom where I have been standing in the doorway listening to what was going on.

I positioned myself at the top of the stairs and sat down. "Annie!" "Adolphus is dead." Mom was about to faint, so the taller policeman held her up and moved her over to the chair and sat her down in it. The wails and screams drew

Roger and Palistine, my cousins, and Delroy from their rooms pass me and down the stairs and into the arms of Aunt Emily Lee and Mom. I remained at the top of the stairs. My attention had been directed toward the happenings in the living room.

The door had been left fully opened not being closed because of all of the excitement. The doorbell rang. Once, twice, three times. The sound drawing my attention back to the door, there in the lighted doorway stood Uncle Adolphus, standing there smiling. He waved and turned, walked down the stairs. I was distracted when mom and the police officers ran toward the front door of the house. The police ran out through the open door and down the stairs. When they reached the sidewalk, the shorter one told the taller one, "Go that way!" 'I'll go this way!" "They couldn't have gotten far." "You go that way" he called out and they ran in opposite directions looking for whom they thought could be ringing the bell. Mom called out.

"What the hell are you looking at?" Once she noticed me sitting at the top of the stairs. "It was Uncle Adolphus Mom." "I saw him standing there in the doorway." I said. Mom looked like all the blood had drained out of her face. She lowered her head and turned to walk back into the living room. "What did he say Annie?" Aunt Emily Lee inquired. Barely getting the words out between deep heaving sobs. "He said that it was Adolphus." "Adolphus?" Aunt Emily Lee questioned. Emotionally broken by the news of her brother's death, Mom answered. "Yes Adolphus!"

Mom and Aunt Emily Lee walked out of the living room and stood at the bottom of the stairs mute, no longer crying, looking up at me, even when the police ran into the house through the front door and out of breath. They never diverted their stare away from me. "Is everything alright?" The shorter of the two asked them, "Ladies!" Again and again, "Ladies!" he screamed each time more earnestly. "Is everything alright?" "We didn't find anybody." We didn't see anybody at all. "It's not possible." The shorter one continued. "Nobody could have gotten away that fast." The taller directed his question to Mom. His questioning was far more calm and controlled than the shorter officer. "Is everything alright?"

Mom was still staring at me, never turning to face the officer. As if with one voice she and Aunt Emily Lee replied at the same time, "We don't know." What I did next was stand up, smile and wave and went back to bed. Whatever occurred the rest of the night and the days that followed, I have no memory of. As hard as I may try, I just can't remember.

What I remember next is being at the funeral home, banging on the glass that covered my Uncle Adolphus, begging him to wake up. He didn't look like he was sleeping at all. There was a smile on his face and moisture on one side of his forehead, the left side of his head if memory serves me right. He just looked like he was laying there smiling with his eyes closed, sweating. That's what I remember, just as though it happened yesterday.

Maybe it was because of my innocence and lack of understanding about death. Wake up, as I look back in retrospect, meant, please, don't go away, please, don't leave me. Other incidents come to mind also. During that short period of time, from the night that we found out he was dead up until the night following his burial. I did not wet the bed.

After the oppressively hot and humid night in Richmond, no one in Mom's family ever again looked at me the same. Not that any of them ever really cared for me in the first place. They just grew more distant from me and far crueler in their treatment of me. Throughout the entire period all but one member of the family treated me as though I wasn't there. That's when I noticed, for what was the first time, Mom's baby brother, Emory Thomas.

Prior to the day of the funeral and burial I don't remember ever having seen or having met him. My first memory of him was that day. He was shorter the Uncle Adolphus and darker. His voice was deep and he was soft spoken. The sadness that he felt inside was apparent on his face. What made his demeanor stand out was his calmness in all the pain and sorrow that permeated the day.

The incident that stayed with me occurred

when all the adult relatives and friends and the children had dressed and were milling about beside the car's that had lined the road outside of my grandparents' house. There must have been thirty cars. For reasons unknown to me to this day, I was not allowed to attend the funeral that was to take place at Little Zion Church. The family had been members there for generations.

Beside and to the left of the front of the church was where he going to be buried in one of the family plots that had been purchased. All were ill prepared for him being placed in one of them so prematurely. Often, Big Daddy, as all the grand children called him, would say, "Children bury parents, parents don't bury their children." That's why plots had been brought.

The burden of selecting a final resting place for him and Big Ma had been taken care of by him; his intent was not to bury one of his children in one of them. Anyway, as I have already stated, for some reason or reasons I was not welcomed to attend. Mom had ordered me to stay in the yard until after the ceremony. At 3 1/2 years old I was very independent and the times were different. Safety was not an issue. I would just do as I was told.

Often my cousins William Edward and C.C., Delroy and I would use some of the old tires as items of play. We would roll them with our hands through the yards and up and down the dirt road in front of the house. So, in order to entertain myself during their absence, I rolled out a tire into the road and watched as everybody loaded into the cars. The tire was as tall as I was. Standing in the road, I propped my back against the tire placing my left foot in the inner tube well.

As you have already been informed, no one had spoken to me since that night in Richmond. Again looking back in time, I have vivid memory of how hot the day was. There had been no wind. Then suddenly, out of nowhere there appeared a small dust whirlwind. It began at the rear of the Hearst that held the body of my Uncle. It swirled around the members of the family blowing off the hats of both the men and woman but never touching them. It swirled rose and fell the length of the road toward me. Everyone stood looking at me as it worked its way down the road. There was no other breeze blowing, just the dust whirlwind.

Uncle Emory had just exited the front door turned toward me and stood stone still looking at me. The whirlwind, that was no higher than four or so feet, left the ground and positioned itself right above my head; I don't remember having any sensation of the blowing wind, swirling dust and grit one would expect from such an odd occurrence. It just enveloped me and swirled around me from head to feet exiting on the road at the base of my feet then slowly dispatched from the top of my head and ceased to exist on the road at the base of my feet.

Friends and family had all ran up the road toward me to view the strange phenomenon.

None approached me, except Uncle Emory. He walked down the road from in front of house toward me. Upon reaching me he placed his hand on the top of my head and messed up my hair. "Do you know who I am?" He asked "Nope!" "I don't." I said. "I'm your Uncle Emory." "See you when I get back." He patted me on the head, turned and walked toward the crowd that had gathered to watch what had just taken place with the dust whirlwind. He walked through them as they parted like the red sea at his approach.

As he passed them they emptied to his rear like water going down a drain and got into their assigned cars. As the hearse pulled onto and down the dusty road, the rest followed en-route to the final resting place of my Uncle Adolphus. I rolled my tire down the road behind the last car until it reached the railroad tracks, then turned and rolled it back up to the house and into the yard. There I leaned it against the old red house that was across the yard from my grandparents' house, my favorite parking place, walked onto the lawn and sat in the brightly painted red metal lawn chair. The grass was deep green despite the heat. The flowers that rimmed the entire lawn enveloped me in sweet fragrances of each flower giving off its own delightful scent.

Sitting there, I could see and hear the children playing and running about the yard, the sounds of the hogs in the pen rooting and snorting, doing what hogs do, just being hogs. What I could not do, for the life of me, was remember the sound of Uncle Adolphus's voice. What did he sound like? I thought over and over again. I, to this day still have no memory of it. What I have never forgotten was the first time that I heard Uncle Emory's voice. Though long, I do still, for some memory of the sound of Uncle Adolphus's. What did he sound like? I thought over and over again. I, to this day, still have no memory of it. Though long I do still for some memory of the sound of Uncle Adolphus. It eludes me. The sound of Uncle Emory's voice had brought to me a level of inner peace. That remembrance of it, throughout my life, made me stronger whenever I considered becoming weak. And whenever failure seemed my only option it drove me to succeed.

As I write this. It, I know, does warrant a more detailed explanation concerning what transpired after the funeral and burial. I am also aware that the reader, you, should be more greatly informed of more of the details. My desire is not to conform to the norm but to tell you tidbits of incidents that led to who and what I have become. Never the less, so as not to leave you in total suspense I will leave you with this much. Upon everyone's return from the funeral and burial, there existed among them an air of disdain for me. That night I wet the bed.

No mention was ever again made concerning what had transpired in Richmond on that faithful night, nor was any mention ever made concerning the dust whirlwind. Not until I was 14 years old. Within weeks my mother, brother, sister and I have boarded a train back to New York. I don't remember anything about the trip. When we arrived in New York we moved in with Aunt Lola. Bringing me to invite you to, just in case you missed it the first time, re-read the portion where I wrote in some detailed tidbits about Aunt Lola and my association with her.

For now it is important to take you back to where I left off. It was my growing friendship with Gut, my un-waving desire to seek, and find comfort in the mirror with the razor. Before I do, however, let me tell you that it was three years from the moment that Uncle Emory said that he would see me when he got back, that I saw him again. We were still living at Aunt Lola's. There was a knock on the door. I opened it. There before me stood Uncle Emory dressed in a Marine Tropical uniform with his barracks cover pulled down so that the brim covered his eyes.

"Hi Bobby, remember me?" He said. Then he removed his barracks cover and placed it on my head. The hat fell and covered both my eyes and ears. "I didn't know then that the uniform and the hat would one day play a major role in my life. "Uncle Emory." I yelled. "Mom, its Uncle Emory." The very sight of him standing there with creases as Sharpe as a razors edge, in his shirt and trousers left an impression on me that lasted all of my life. His shoe's gleaming like varnished wood on his feet, made me want to fall to my knees and worship him as a beautiful bronze

God.

Mom was overjoyed to see him. After spending time going over lost times with her and getting to know my new baby sister Katie, who had been born during their separation. He took Delroy and me down to Mom's grocery store across the street on the downtown side of 117th street and Madison Avenue. At that time Madison Avenue was a two way street running both up and down town. I was in awe of just being able to walk beside him, in step, in his shadow. I'll never forget that day.

At Mom's store he reached into the ice filled soda cooler that sat beside the entrance. He drew from within it two brown iced bottles of Dad's root beer. Popped the cap and handed one to Delroy, the other to me. The bottle was so cold that I could not hold it in either hand for very long. So I shifted it continuously from one hand to the other. After paying Mom for the drinks and a pack of cigarettes, the three of us, walked back out into the brightly lit sunny day.

Uncle Emory tore open the cigarette pack from a bottom corner with his teeth. Removed one and placed the pack into the top of his left sock on the inside portion. Without breaking the match from its book, he folded it over and with his thumb struck it and lit his cigarette. I watched and was mindful of his every move. Remember, I told you that I was and am a watcher. Once we reached the stoop at 51 East 117th street where we lived. Uncle Emory paused, took the last few puffs from his cigarette and flicked it away with the fingers of his right hand. He was magnificent in his being and his every movement.

From that day forward, I was determined to become a Marine. Determined, I was, to become Uncle Emory in every manner and detail. One day, I said to myself, I too am going to be just as magnificent. Even though I had drank Dad's root beer before, it was, you must know, my favorite drink. Never before had it tasted so well nor has it since. The one that Uncle Emory brought for me that day had a flavor all its own. One might venture to say that, to me it tasted like it had been sweetened with love.

There remains nothing in my memory as to how long he stayed after our return or at what time of the day or evening he departed. I suppose it was blocked out of my mind. What I heard, by way of conversation among the adults was that he had been transferred and was stationed in Japan, when next I saw him it was two years later and we were at that time living on 129th street.

During that visit he taught me how to spit shine shoes. We talked about my education and my desire to join the Marines. Uncle Emory slept on the living room sofa that night. That night I did not wet the bed. I did not sleep either. When all were in restful slumber I eased from my bed and went into the living room where I sat in the chair beside the sofa. From the chair, I guarded him throughout the night. Not returning to my bed until the sky started to take on the glow of the first light of the dawn. Little did I realize then how close I was to taking the first step toward my becoming him, my uncle Emory.

The only thing that needed to be done was to find a way to stay alive a, way to escape, and a place to escape to. The Marine Corps seemed to be the most likely route. There, I supposed, I would just be another Marine. As equal as any other young man willing to serve honorably and with the dignity expected of him.

There no one would beat me. As a Marine, I would at last have found a place to belong. It would be wonderful to be able to dip my hands into the sands of time and from it sift out all of the unhappy times of my existence, all of those grains of sand that hold anger, despair, and hate. I would let seep through my fingers, leaving only those that harbored happiness, and thus relieving me of those times of my life over and over again, on into eternity.

The memories of Uncle Adolphus would not be what could possibly be the imagination of a child. All the beatings would fade from my memory, as would be the memories of the razor and the mirror. All of those instants in time measured by grains of sand falling back into the seas of time washed away forever. No more craving to be completely relieved of a gnawing pain that ate away at me like a cancer. Like a cancer eating away at my heart, little by little consuming the very center of my being, all that was me inside, slowly ever so slowly, but destroying me nonetheless.

My most earnest desire, for the moment was to get to Gut's house, to just sit and talk about anything and everything. No limits to where he and I could go to rid ourselves of where we were now, a place of peace and friendly conversation. A place where make believe becomes reality. A place where little boys, rather than walk they skip and chuckle with joy and glee. Where life is now and there are no yesterdays, only now and tomorrow.

Each day, in my normal life cycle, born anew, brought the normal morning beating. My days' were filled with the same despair and dread, my nights somber and dark. Nightmares of life's events tormented me. One would think that the growling and pain in my innards due to lack of food would shock me out of my tortured slumber. Then there was the stinging pain that I endured caused by the salt in my urine eating away at the tenderness of my childish flesh. The wetness of my covers and mattress, should, you would think, make it uncomfortable enough to render me unable to fall off into sleep.

But, oh, how wrong your thoughts of what you consider the norm. The situation was normal for me. It was normal for me to lay there in the darkness, it being penetrated only by the flicking glow of the television in Mom and Pops room, and by the light that escaped from the windows of our neighbors and bounced about the walls of the garage filled airshaft that divided the two adjoined buildings, sixty and sixty two.

The filth and stench in which I lay was a breeding ground for the roaches that found their way up the walls and through the cracks in the baseboards that lacked of proper maintenance and that time and created. Strange bedfellows they were not. They were as all else vile and comfortable aspects in my life, simply the norm.

Sometimes in the still of the night, through the airshaft I could hear conversations varied in context. Sometimes moans emitted in the throngs of passion. Heated and vulgar arguments brought on by the over consumption of a taste too many of Gin, beer and cheap wine.

There was even conversation about me. "Did you smell that boy when he walked past you in the hallway?" One voice breaking the silence of the night would ask. In response the other said, "How can they do that to a child?" "He is such a pitiful sight." "The poor thing, I hear that they don't even feed him half the time, what's he doing eating from the trash?" The first voice said. The other continued, "At least he don't scream like he used to when they be beating his ass."

"Shame, damn shame, they gonna kill that child." "Doesn't anybody love him at all?" You have just answered your own question, I thought to myself. Though I was driven to jump out of bed, run to the window and lean out and yell at the top of my lungs.

"Doesn't anybody love this child?" I just

restrained myself, I having become the master of restraint, and in the darkness I wondered, why. I welled up with emotion, then released the floodgates and cried silently. I stuffed the filthy wet blanket into my mouth so that no sound would emerge and prompt my father to investigate. What I didn't want to do was provoke his rage. The fact that I would dare to interrupt his sleep with a display of heartfelt emotion would only have brought a beating.

How dare I attempt to bring to anyone's attention that I was in fact, a human being. Nor did I want to wake up Delroy. Without a doubt he would have eased out of his bed, as though he was going to the bathroom, and edged his way to Pop's side of the bed and whispered to Pop that I woke him up.

That's the kind of sneak that he was. Let us not forget the pleasure he would have gotten while watching Pop beat all hell out of me. During those periods, my emotional pain was always replaced with fear and despair. I would, sometime during those emotional ups and down's, fall off into fitful sleep. I would awake wet in the morning. Nothing, as I have already told you, ever changed. My every day's and all of my tomorrows were just as my yesterdays.

To say that I was suffering from some form of depression would be an understatement. The nail in my coffin came on a bright spring morning. The rays of the sun broke through the front room window like yellow bands of gold. I could hear the roar and rumble of the Department of Sanitation street cleaner truck as it passed by our building, the brushes churning and water spraying from its bowels. I could almost see the rainbow in its spray; I could smell the foulness of the gutter as it was churned up by the massive thick bristles of the brushes, the wonderful and distinct sounds and smells of New York City.

I could have gotten lost in it all had it not been for the vile wetness in which I lay, if it had not been for the fear, and the dread welling up inside of me. I was waiting to be pulled from my bed and beaten. To my amazement he got up, dressed and walked out the front door. Had by chance my prayers had been answered? Was I invisible? I dared not tempt fate. I lay still as a church mouse being stalked by a cat. My breath became shallow. I tried to still the fast loud beating of my heart; rotating ever so slowly I turned face down in my bed. At a snails pace I moved to the covers over my shoulders, neck and covered my head.

Safe and secure in my own mind I lay motionless and silent. Wondering all the time when and how the attack would come, but after what seemed like hours, in fact less than one, it never came. Had he found me dead therefore having no need to violate a corpse? No, I was alert and my senses where operational. Life was apparent. Besides, the stench was not what I expected to experience in heaven. Hell, I think not. I was already in occupancy of that domain.

Maybe he just didn't want to exert the effort this morning I thought, surely upon his return. I waited.

In fact it was ten o'clock when my mother got out of bed. She came to the side of my bed as if driven and with clothes line in hand began to tie my ankles to the bed. "Wake up you little fuck." "Wake the hell up." She screamed. "Please Mom, Please!" I begged. "Get your hands and legs at the corners of the bed, now!" She said while at the same time that she was talking she was yanking my arms toward the head of the bed.

Though I was filled with a fear of what was going to take place, I complied. She tied my waist to the corners of the headboard and without another word she walked back into her bedroom. She was opening and closing closets and drawers, cursing in a rage as she searched and hunted for whatever it was that she was seeking.

I didn't want to know and was sorry that I had wondered. The old pains that I had experienced in the past, would, that day become a memory that I would come to crave and remember as slight, in it's infliction. Her breathing, when she came back and stood beside my bed, was labored. She could barely speak when she commanded Delroy, Edie and Katie to go into the living room. Delroy snickered and poked me in the head as he left. What did she have in mind for me? I wondered. What instruments had she gathered to punish me with?

Did I really want to know? Yes! No! I cried silently though deeply into my covers.

The coldness that abject fear brings engulfed me. Terror is a better way to describe what ran rampart through me. The memory of the man with the hanger was, for the moment, a reminder of what she was capable of doing to me, was a constant on my mind. "Goldie will be here in a while, and then we'll see just how much you want to fuck up my marriage and my life." She said panting and shaking the bed. "Answer me while you can you little fuck." "You're going to get something this mother fucking day that you never dreamed of or read in one of those books." "Uh-huh that's right."

That's when one of the items she choose came crashing down across my back. Boom! I screamed as the leg from the card table impacted into the arch of my back. "God, my God Mommy, my God." I pleaded. "What did I do?" "Please Mommy, what did I do?" I cried. "You live and breathe." She yelled. "You live and breathe, that's what you do." "Your daddy walked out this morning because he didn't want to dirty his hands on you." "When I send you to the store, you go to the store that I send you to." "Not where the hell you want to go."

She ranted, she continued. "When I send you to Barney's, that's where I want you to go." "Breath hard, you bastard, breathe deep, you're going to need it." "Today, you smart little bastard, may be the last time you breath the same air as

me." She said without changing the expression of loathing and contempt on her face. From the living room I could hear Mighty Mouse sing, "Here I come to save the day."
"That means that Mighty Mouse is on his way."

It was a childish song for children searching for a hero, nothing more. There would be no Mighty Mouse to save my day. I held my breath so that I could die before cousin Goldie arrived, but I couldn't die. I couldn't hold my breath long enough. My dread was soon intensified moments later when there was a knocking at the door. "Annie, Annie, it's me Goldie." I prayed that it would all be over soon. That he would just cut my throat and I would bleed out on to the filth and stench of my existence and at last find peace and comfort in the arms of a God, the God who during my short life rejected me. I prayed. "Dear God." "If you are there and if you are real?" "Please don't let it hurt too much." "Please give me a sign that you are there and that you hear me."

There came to be no sign from God, only cousin Goldie peering down on me. His eyes as cold as steel staring into mine reflecting the coldness in his heart, the hatred that dwelled deep there within them for me, hatred, I could not understand. "I got this Annie." Cousin Goldie said. "His ass is mine." Laying there defenseless and frightened witless, I had no idea what they had planned for me. "I can't stand your pissy ass, you little motherfucker." "Think about how hell is going to feel while you're dying." Goldie growled.

He then grabbed me around my neck and began to choke me. As I fought for air, he wrapped my head in the covers and began to smother me. Blackness began to enclose on me. At the moment when I thought that death had at last embraced me, the impact of some object striking me between my shoulder blades brought me back from the brink of what would have proven to be the only peace I could have ever known, death. The sweetness and comfort of its caress was not mine to process. The pleasures of simplicity continued to elude me.

Surely by now, as the reader, you must have come to the conclusion that ever so slowly I was going mad. Beaten, humiliated and tortured into a mental state from which no human being could ever recover. As the reader, please understand that for creatures like me. Death would be the only cure. Man will never discover a pill or an injection that would rid me, and those like me, of this desire to be destroyed or to destroy one self. I and those like me are blights upon all that is normal and reasonable to mankind.

Those like me finding relief only in the pain that we can inflict on ourselves. We are abandoned by the reality of it all, engulfed by the fantasy we create in such escapes such as my own, the mirror and the razor. Cut away what others see and what is recreated and reborn is what others want you to be. Just like them, even though we can never be what others want us to be.   Nor can I, nor those like me, ever be, just like them. I and those like me are and remain forever innocent, unblemished, and unsacred by the hate, envy and guilt experienced by what is normal for all those who are contributors to the moral and social ills of the world.

No, we find comfort with bits of broken glass, which we embed in, or cut away at our own private parts. The sharpness of a silvery or rusted sewing needle or safety pin thrust into the abdomen, or the upper and lower lip. We have bald spots in our heads caused by twisting and yanking our hair out by their roots.

Experts we are at the intentional creation of minor accidents, like crushing our fingers in doors or drawers, accidental falls head first into a wall. Falls from our bikes, or our roller skates were gifts from above. They provided the means by which to obtain deep scrapes and scratches on our knees and elbows, injuries that we could conceal as we picked and dug in them for weeks.

The instrument of choice, it seems. The one that brought the most pleasure and allowed you the most delightful of results was the razors, single edge, or double edge, to each, his or her own. The face, abdomen, arms, legs, we all have choices. It's all about a matter of choice for us, whatever the device, the method, the tool or choice of body part. It all boiled down to what choice we made that would deliver the kind of relief we were seeking.

I lived in a world that consisted of logic and

reasoning, black or white, right or wrong. Never shades of gray, no shadows, only light or dark. No may be's or could be's, would ahh's could ahh's or should ahh's. Only I will or I won't. With us it is only a truth or a lie.

We are incapable of feeling the emotion hate as far as other human beings might. We are consumed with such a loathing and hatred for our own existence that this one, of few, emotions experienced by the so-called norm is reserved just for ourselves. You must look deep in order to see and understand what lies beneath the genius child. In a noted poem by Langston Hughes he wrote, "Nobody loves a genius child?" "Kill him and let his soul run wild."

Mom and Cousin Goldie were in the process of proving that on that morning. Mom emerged from the bedroom with a diaper. She crammed it into my mouth so that my screams would be silenced. It was soiled and I could taste the urine and feces.

The beating continued. The verbal abuse was relentless. "Don't leave any marks Goldie," Mom said. "Then put some more shit over his head Annie." "I want to punch this motherfucker in his face." Cousin Goldie replied. Mom complied by running into her bedroom and retrieving a pillow from her bed and putting it over my head. Bam, Bam, Bam, the blows seemed as though my head was being driven through the mattress and the rusted supports and hangers that held my bed together, I began to gag and vomit.

The vomit, because of the diaper that had been stuffed into my mouth, was not able to come out of my mouth. So the only exit that it had was through my nose. It burned and I choked and cried in muffled screams. I could feel my face puff and swell. My nose began to bleed and the metallic taste of blood overpowered my sense of taste. Each time that he struck me with his closed fist the sound intensified and the impact drove me deeper into a neither world of shades of gray rather than complete blackness that would have proven to be a welcome reprieve from my tormentors.

The sound of Cousin Goldie flicking open his knife sent shivers up my spine. "Let me stick it in him just this much Annie." "Please!" He begged. "I'll stick it where nobody can see it." Mom asked, "You sure that you can stick it in just that much?" "Sure," Cousin Goldie said. "Right here under his shoulder blade." "His shirt will cover it." "Annie I just got to stick this motherfucker." "You know how long I've been waiting to do this?" "If I can't kill his ass, at least let me stick him a couple of times," he whined. "Stick his ass Goldie, "Stick him!" My mother replied. I felt the point of the knife against my back where there is a separation between the shoulder blade and the indentation in the back.

At first he just spun the point in a circle. "That's it. Yeah that's it." "Some blood is coming out of this little mother fucker." "Yeah, some blood is coming out." He spoke very slowly and deliberately as he twirled the point into my flesh. "I'd like to cut his nuts off Annie." "Then he could never make another motherfucker like him." Then I felt the pressure. Slowly he inserted the blade into my back. At first there was no pain. Then I could feel it, the burning sharp pain. I could feel my eyes expand to the size of dinner plates. The vomit and blood in my mouth gushed out of my nose as the scream tried to escape from my innermost parts to become a mournful wail, a vocal plea for help.

Each time I would emit a wail Delroy and my sisters would mimic me and giggle. Mom would, each time, yell for them to shut up. They never the less got great pleasure and found an abundance of humor in my pain. I was alone.

What I had to do was endure until the end. However or whenever that may take place, in my heart of hearts I prayed that it would be soon. For what seemed like hours they beat me with the cord from the iron, a razor strap and shoes. I think they stopped simply because they grew tired. The ties that bound me spread eagle and face down had rubbed deep into my wrist and ankles. They burned once combined with my own sweat. My back, legs and arms throbbed from the beating.

Panting and still enraged, Cousin Goldie leaned close to my face and said, "Have a good day motherfucker." "The next time I'll kill your little ass." Without saying another word he slammed the door behind him and he was gone.

Mom came to the side of the bed and yanked the diaper out of my mouth. The vomit and blood soaked the blanket and sheets. "Get your self ready to go to the store," she commanded. "This time go where I send you." She untied me but I was not able to move. Arms and legs still extended I lay motionless sobbing.

Having not eaten in five days the vomit was green from the bile and streaked with red blood from the punches inflicted on me by Cousin Goldie. The punches left both my mouth and nose bloody. My left eye was almost swollen shut. Their attempt to leave no marks had failed. I was visual proof of that.

As always I would explain it away as injuries sustained while playing roughly during another unprotected football game. Did people believe me? I don't know. What I came to know though, was that no one cared; no one wanted to get involved. It was easy to be blind to what was happening to me, easy to be deaf to the cries of an abused child. And the silence was deafening. The isolation was leading me closer to despair and more deeply depressed.

While I dressed, having to endure the snickers and sneers of my siblings was hard to tolerate. As I dressed, they ate. There was no doubt in my mind which store she was going to send me to. The very idea that I would have to come face to face with the fat man with the large distorted, deformed large eye, embraced me like the cold of winter. I shook and shivered in the warm sunlight breaking through the front window.

I was tempted to tell my mother what he had done to me. Tempted I said. You see she would not have cared anyway and it would just have caused me more embarrassment, and another beating. I lived in a world where I didn't matter. No one cared and no one was going to help me. How could someone so little and tiny be expected to be so strong. On the inside I was so fragile, so weak, so empty, so lonely and lost. I was afraid.

"Get two pounds of ground beef." "Two pounds of bacon sliced thick and a nice chicken." Mom continued. "If you have any change left spend it on some potatoes." "What ever the change will buy, if you hadn't made me hurt my hand this morning I would have written a list." "Don't matter though, you're a smart ass, you can remember." "You'd better remember!" Mom handed me five dollars and fifty cents. Opened the front door and with an underhand motion waved me out into the hallway.

This spring day, warmed by the new sun of the season would provoke any little child to want to skip and play. The definitive words being, "any little child," I wasn't. I was battered and abused. The sun caused my eye to ache. There was so much pain in my face and back that I wanted to fall to my knees and crawl. Putting up a front had become a normal part of my life by now. So that's what I did, though barely. Rather than walk up the block toward Madison Avenue. I choose to go down to Park Avenue and walk under the elevated train tracks. Even on the brightest of days, it was always dark beneath them.

The chance that I would come across any other person was remote if not next to zero. Without being able to gain access to a mirror, I had a pretty good idea what I must have looked like. When I ran my hand over my face it felt sore and bloated.

The part of my life that I loved the most, because I had a beautiful voice, was singing, I found that the swelling of my lips made it almost impossible, but I sang anyway as I walked beneath the train tracks in the shadows. My speech though distorted did not prevent the birds from envying me. "He's got the whole world, in his hands, "He's got the whole world in his hands." "He's got the whole world in his hands; he's got the whole world in his hands." I sang beautifully.

My singing, for the moment, soothed away the fear of the fat man with the distorted big eye. Looking up 128th street, from Park Avenue toward Madison Avenue, the street seemed to expand in its length. Stretching off into the far distant horizon, the more I walked the further away Madison Avenue seemed to get. The block would collapse in on itself, and then seemed to expand. There was no longer a song in my heart, only fear and apprehension.

From the corner of 128th street and

Madison I could see Berney's. Mr. Taylor who owned the grocery store next to Berney's was sitting out front talking to Dr. Mills the gentleman who owned the drug store. Dr. Mills would later on in my life play a very important role in helping me to escape from my parents and family. Avoiding them was going to be impossible so I walked up and in a happy tone of voice said, "Good morning Mr. Taylor, Dr. Mills."

Mr. Taylor looked at me and then at Dr. Mills. They both responded almost at the same second. "Hey Bobby, how's our boy doing today?" "What happened to your face?" Mr. Taylor asked. "Nothing sir, nobody hit me, I was just playing foot...." Before I could finish my sentence Dr. Mills interrupted. "Bobby, nobody asked you did anybody do anything to you, just what happened." "Maybe football just isn't your game." "Come on into the store so that I can clean you up." I waved at Mr. Taylor and said "See you later."

Shaking his head Mr. Taylor stood up and said "Bobby, boy they mean to kill you, sho as I as loves my coffee likes I loves my women, black and sweet." "Baby boy they gonna kill you." While raising his right arm toward the sky and shaking his head, he walked into his grocery store. Muttering, "God help his poor little soul." "Jesus weep, Jesus weep." Dr. Mills extended his left arm and pulled my head to his side and wrapped it around me. I wanted to pull away because it hurt so badly, but it felt so good to be held.

So I leaned against him and with my eyes closed walked with him into the drug store. We walked right in front of Berney's and so lost, I was in the comfort of his loving kindness, I never opened my eyes; I never even saw the store. Dr. Mills took me back behind the counter. He took a box of cotton from the shelf and un-rolled it placing it on the table. Then he got a bottle of something from another shelf and placed that on the table next to the cotton. "Sing something for me son, sing something nice." He asked.

"Every time I hear a new born baby cry, or touch a leaf, or see the sky. Then I know why. I believe." I sang softly. "That's beautiful child. He said. "Now this will burn just a little when you swish it around in your mouth, but don't spit it out until I tell you to." "Ok, sure Dr. Mills," I said. So it did burn but I swished anyway until he told me to spit it out into the sink. "Sing some more, child." So I sang some more as he cleaned and patted my face will the cotton with whatever was in the bottle soaking it. Each time I would wince he would say, "Sing sweet child." "Sing." I sang. "If everyone lit just one little candle, what a bright world this would be."

Tears welled up in Dr. Mills's eyes, but he fought them back, saying. "My poor boy, my poor little boy how can anybody hurt such a nice child like you." "Every time I see you you've got a smile on your face, even after you've had another bad day playing football, you have a smile on your face." "What do you do with the money that you make running errands for me and everybody else?" "Let me help you." "I'll do anything that I can do for you." "Tell me how I can help you." "Please!" "Dr. Mills." I said. "I'm fine." "Thanks for taking care of me and cleaning me up." "But I have to go." "I'm fine." "Really I'm fine."

What prompted me to take his hand into mine and kiss it, I'll never know. However that's what I did. No longer able to maintain his composure Dr. Mills let the tears flow. The bell above the door rang as I opened it and rang as it closed behind me. I exited to enter into the real world, my world where there was no compassion, no pity, my world where I was prey.

Mr. Berney was cutting liver into slices as I entered. The fat man was not sitting on his stool. "What you need little Red?" (That's what Mr. Berney called me). As fast as I could I blurted out, "2 pounds ground beef, 2 pounds of thick sliced bacon and a nice chicken." "Please!" "That'll be 2 pounds of ground beef, what else did you say?" He asked while writing on a piece of brown butcher paper. "Mr. Berney, 2 pounds of ground beef, 2 pounds of thick sliced bacon and a nice chicken." I responded. "I got ya little Red."

From the back of the store I heard him. "Is that my little friend out there?" It was the fat man. I froze where I was, though my first impulse was to run I just couldn't. "As he walked in from the back he repeated himself, "Is that my little friend?" That smile and that eye and the smell of the raw meat brought back horrible memories of what he had done to me. I didn't answer him. What I did was divert my eyes to the sawdust on the floor and started kicking it over the toes of my U.S. Keds sneakers.

Time went by slowly as Mr. Berney put my order together. I continued to ignore the fat man, but he kept talking to me, kept trying to get me to make some kind of contact with him. "That'll be four dollars and fifteen cent Little Red." Looking up I saw Mr. Berney finish his addition on the brown butcher paper and stick the pencil behind his right ear, "four dollars and fifteen cent," he said again. "Do you need anything thing else my boy?" Mr. Berney asked. "No sir, nothing else except eighty-five cents worth of white potatoes." I replied. "You got to get those over there my boy." Mr. Berney said. "Over there," pointing toward the fat man sitting on his stool.

He had a smile on his face like one would expect to see on the face of the cat that ate the canary. "Berney, I don't have them out yet." "He'll have to go with me to the back to get them." The fat man said stepping down from his perch on the stool. "C'mon let's go into the back, we'll pick out some nice ones." The fat man said, "Never mind we don't need them." I responded, "Yes you do, otherwise your father and mother wouldn't have told you to get them." "Maybe I'll just ask him when he comes pass," was his reply. There was no door leading to the back of the store, just a curtain.

He led and I followed. It was dimly lit and there were crates of fruits and vegetables stacked neatly against the walls. There were also large silver tins labeled in bright large red letters, "Lard." "If you want these taters sweetie you've got to make me happy." "You know what it takes to make me happy." He moaned while stepping closer and closer to me as I backed up against the crates of vegetables.

"Drop them baby." "Let me see that sweet little ass." He said, while unzipping his pants and taking out his already erected penis. Crying and pleading I begged. "Please don't hurt me." "Just let me go home, please." Ignoring my pleas he said, "This time it won't hurt I have something for that." "This time I'll take my time up in that tight little ass."

He then flipped the lid off of the lard can and taking a generous amount from it he began to rub it up and down his penis. "I'll tell Mr. Berney if you touch me." I cried. "I swear, I'll tell." "I'll tell your father you little bitch." "I'll tell him that you're a nasty little faggot and that you asked me to do it to you." "Who do you think they'll believe me, or a little freak of nature like you?" Was his threat. I tried to run past him but he was able to grab my arm and throw me onto the crates. For a large man he moved very quickly. He then pulled my pants down, and turned me over onto my face. He then spread my buttocks apart and forced himself into me, the entire time saying dirty filthy things as he enjoyed himself while he violated me. When I started to cry out from the pain he reached into a crate of plums and stuffed one into my mouth. "I'm gonna break this tight little ass hole in right." He moaned. "I'm gonna make it mine." "That's my sweet ass." He began to pound himself in me and against me faster and harder.

He squeezed my buttocks tightly together while I continued to squirm in an attempt to get away from him. "It's coming you little bitch, its coming." "Take me!" Take me!" He growled as he ejaculated into me. It hurt and burned so badly that I wanted to die. I felt sick and dirty when he had finished. The beast fell exhausted back onto a crate and reached next to him and retrieved an old dirty apron and wiped the blood and lard from his penis. I sank to the floor stretched out my legs and pulled up my pants. It felt like he had torn my guts out.

"Now sweet ass you can have eighty five cents worth of potatoes," He said while gasping for air. A lifetime later he stood up and packed a brown paper bag with white potatoes and placed them at my feet. Then he just walked out through the curtains and assumed his position on his stool. I picked up the bag of potatoes and followed. Mr. Berney handed me the meat and chicken that I had paid for. Limping and in violent agony I went on my way.

The block was filled with my neighbors walking about and interacting with one another. Some of the guy's were already playing basketball on the makeshift court that we had created on the sidewalk in front of the empty lot beside All Saints Church. The hoop was a round vegetable basket fastened to the fence with wire and clothes hangers. I saw nothing, felt nothing and heard nothing. What I felt was sick.

As was the norm nobody spoke to me directly. Whatever was said about me registered only as, "blah, blah and blah." When I reached my building I started up the steps almost walking over Mrs. Margaret. When I realized that she was there I looked up at her. She stroked the top of my head and just said, "Poor baby, poor little baby," and walked down the steps and away she went down the block toward Park Avenue.

When I had knocked on the door and gained entry into the apartment, I took the meat and potatoes into the kitchen, and then I went into the bathroom removed Pop's razor from the cabinet and began to cut more deeply than I had ever cut before. After I had, in my own mind, cut away enough of the ugly that I was, I went into the living room sat down in the corner next to the window beside the steam pipe, drew my legs up to my chin and cried. For the first time the mirror and the razor brought me no comfort. Hungry, raped and in pain nobody paid me any attention.

They laughed and played and watched television around me. Nobody noticed me or cared to. Their lives went as usual. So did mine. For four more years the fat man with the large eye continued to have his way with me.

Sometimes he would force me to tolerate the pain of anal sex other times he would force himself into my mouth until he ejaculated. As he would say after each rape, "You're my sweet ass little bitch." "I own you." He was right. Who could I tell? Who would help me? Who would believe me? And who really cared?

This is the first time that I have ever shared this horror with anyone, as I have already informed you. For my own peace of mind there will be no further need to venture back to the past and bring up those memories. From this point on those violations will be stored away and never spoken of again. The fact that I had to share those memories with you has brought me to tears. Even after over forty years I remember each incident as though it happened only yesterday.

The story had to be told as it happened, otherwise the story would not be true, and it is the truth that makes the story. I, though, am no longer living in fear of the fat man with the large deformed eye. My only fear now is that I will die alone and that I won't be missed. Adapted to my lot in life is what has happened to me. Over the years my days and nights continued each one as the other.

Gut and I grew ever closer as time moved forward more rapid than either of us could have perceived. Our walks took us further and further from our neighborhood. We explored every aspect of the food world. Gut, I must point out, tended to dive rather than wade into the culinary delights offered up to those who strived to venture into the varied cultural flavors that made up New York City.

Some afternoons we would take the number 1 train to the South Ferry station, get off and board the ferry to Staten Island. Spending countless hours gazing into the murky brown green waters of the East river pretending that we were being deployed to some far off country to land on a beach being riddled by machine gun fire and explosive shells heaped on us by an enemy of great number intent on stopping the wave of freedom from washing up on the shores.

We cast ourselves as heroes of the nation, willing to pay the ultimate price for freedom and the American way of life. Neither of us could have imagined how real the game would play itself out in the near future. Then there were the hours that we spent lying on the slopes of rocky mounds in Mount Morris Park.

Our minds took us to a time when the lady of our dreams embraced us with loving arms. There were names given to the children born only on the clouds that floated high and softly above our heads in a sky that we created, a sky that was always clear and blue. Only warm soft winds blew, and there in and among the wild flowers and heather frolicked the family that we by fate, maybe by design, would never have.

Happiness was our constant companion even when we searched the corner trash cans and the gutters for soda bottles that we would wash in the open hydrants and cash for two and five cents in order to finance our adventures. The best of times were when we, alone in Gut's room, would sit for hours playing records. Gut loved it when I would sing along. "Why do your eyes' roll back in your head every time you sing Bob?" He would ask. I would always tell him that I didn't know, but I did. When my eyes rolled back into my head I could see the music in my heart. Besides that's what Sam Cooke and Jackie Wilson did. I thought it made me look cool.

"Cop your grand Bob!" Gut would say. Cop your grand was one of Gut's signature lines. Even now when I feel the need to be up-lifted I bring up from the memory storage bins of my heart Gut saying, "Cop your grand Bob!" And I am made a little stronger. I am able to survive a little bit longer.

On Sundays, we would watch the picture for a Sunday afternoon or the Million Dollar Movie. There was always the guarantee that we could ride off into the sunset on our trusted swift steeds with the damsel-sitting sidesaddle in our arms. We could kill 100 Japs or Germans with one belt of ammo, locked and loaded into our .30 cal water-cooled machine gun. I could lead my warriors in victory against Custer and his men.

Gut always rooted for the 7th Calvary knowing full well that they lost. I think now that he just liked being difficult. Marching in step with John Payne and Randolph Scott as the Marine

Corps hymn played in the background, sometimes crying with him in Sentimental Journey. The two of us were bound together as brothers of imagination. It was not uncommon to see us walking down the street with our arms around each other, friends without condition. Life outside of my home was wonderful, but short lived.

When Mrs. Gutloff was able to send Gut away to Saint Emma's military school in Virginia, I was alone again. The two of us wrote often. We devised a written code that we knew no one could break. Often I would go by to visit Mrs. Gutloff to relieve both of us of the lonesome feelings that we felt during Gut's absence. She would let me sit in his room and play records.

With Gut gone I would run errands for her, keep her company and wait for the holidays. Time seemed to drag by. The sky wasn't, as blue and warm breezes became cold winds. There was no longer any pleasure found in the tasting of different foods. I only hungered for my friend. During the long period between September and November the grand adventure had ended. Life was not worth exploring. There came to be no mystery worth investigating.

Composing love letters to the girls that attended All Saints School lacked the poetry and fluidness that our two minds could create. What I had little need of when he was around everyday became necessary once again on a regular basis, the razor and the mirror. I began cutting myself more and more each day. Sadly, I moved from not only cutting my face but also my arms and legs were included. Sometimes my shirt and pants would stick to the open cuts, bonding with the drops of blood. My face always looked liked I was on the loosing end of a catfight.

Thanksgiving came not soon enough. When Gut arrived he was sharp in his gray uniform and combat boots. It was apparent that he was not happy. Often in his letters he told me how out of place he felt. How the other students would tease him and ridicule him. It was hard to encourage him. I couldn't touch him so comforting him was impossible. Selfish though it may seem, I only wrote him about how much I missed him.

Mrs. Gutloff knew that we both, Gut and I, were having a hard time dealing with our separation issues. She knew that we were all that each other had. The Thanksgiving weekend went by faster than we had hoped. I had little time to spend with him. Being the holiday and all, we were obligated to spend some time with our own families. I got to spend some time with him on the Sunday morning before he left. We promised to write often and that when he came home for Christmas we would spend more time together, Christmas being a longer break from school. Little did we know that I would be the one missing a year later on Christmas morning.

After that Thanksgiving we would only share two more holiday's together Christmas of 1962 and the fourth of July 1969. By the time Gut left I knew that I had to leave home. The older I got the more brutal the beatings got. I'd grown so tired of the maltreatment, the demeaning verbal abuse and the lack of love and compassion. Escape was my only option. The question was, escape to where, and to what? Where didn't matter as long as it was away from where I was, and to what could not be any worse than here.

During Gut's absence my depression became worse. I cut myself just about every day. Seeking other methods to rid myself of the me my family didn't like. I turned to licking small portions of rat poison, taking a spray or two of raid into my mouth, running in front of cars speeding down Madison Avenue. I was eventually struck five times by cars and buses. Each time limping away at a fast pace before the police or help could arrive. Consuming the poison left me weak and sick all of the time. There were seizures and vomiting constantly. I would vomit so much that I was always dehydrated.

Though, most of the time I was in a horrible condition, the beatings went on without let up. Not a day went by when I didn't stink to the high heavens. To make the stench go away I would use the pine cleaner that Mom kept for cleaning the bathroom and pour a little in my hands and rub it into my body. It burned when coming in contact with the open sores and wounds that they or I had inflicted on me. Rather than cover up the stench of urine it only lent to create a new more offensive one, Pissy-Pine.

Departing from my world was non-existent. I had no social skills, no ability to interact with children of my own age. Adults were repulsed by my persona, too young to be acting so old and set in my ways. It wasn't that I didn't want to skate or ride a bike. Play hide and go seek, Chutes and Ladders, ping-pong or even skellies. I just didn't know how. I'd rather read the works of Walt Whitman and Poe. Watch the graceful moves of Joan Crawford as she floated across the screen about to engage in dramatic dialog with Zachary Scott. Words, when Gut was not around, were my playmates.

My love of words and their application always permitted me to compose unsigned love letters to beautiful young girls who shared them with other girls who in turn shared them with others. Josephine once asked me did I know who her unknown lover was. As she read it to me she began to choke and cry softly. The volume in her voice changed from normal to a soft whimpering whisper. "Have you ever heard anything so lovely?" Josephine asked after reading the letter in it entirety. "Oh, I wish I could find out who he is." "I'll bet he's handsome with light skin and curly hair."

She moaned while pressing the letter to her still forming breast, I never bothered to tell her that it was I. Why distort her vision of what her secret prince looked like? Why destroy her dream. Here I was ugly, red skinned with unkept hair? "No Joe, I have no idea who could have written something that nice." I said, "Someone capable of bringing together such words of beauty would have nothing to do with me, you know that Joe." As she wiped away a tear from the corner of her eye, her head slightly bent forward. A half smile crossed her faced. She said, "Bobby, do you think that I am cute?" "Yes I replied." "I think that you are beautiful." "I know you and when you aren't running down the street or crossing it to avoid me." "Don't we talk and spend time together?" I nodded, "yes." That makes us friends and I'll bet that if you weren't hiding so much of you from other people, you would be able to write letters more lovely than this."

"I know that there is a loving heart underneath those clothes your parents make you wear and someone sweet and gentle." "We girls know those kinds of things Bobby." "Never have I teased you or found reasons not to talk to you." "Don't you think that I smell the same odors as everyone else?" When they call you a freak I defend you by telling them that all you are is different." "Take the time one day and write me a letter." Then she turned and went into the building.

The letter to Josephine was written on November 11th, 1992, thirty years after that exchange, I didn't have her address, so I never mailed it. Josephine and I have never again seen each other. Her dreams are still in tact. To this day she has no idea that her prince was really a toad. I signed it, "Your loving friend, Bobby."

One morning after I had completed my daily chores; I decided to go for a walk downtown. After walking for what seemed an eternity I found myself on Times Square off of 42nd street. There on an island in the middle stood a small building painted blue and white and red. Outside was a poster of a United States Marine on it standing at parade rest in Dress Blues.

When I crossed over I noticed six or seven young boys sitting inside. So I entered and sat down beside them. They looked at one another and moved a few seats over. I suppose it was to escape the odor that I emitted. "Hi, young man my name is Gunnery Sergeant Fitzgerald how can I help you." "Sir," I responded, "I want to be a Marine; I want to join today and leave today." Smiling, he said, "Son, it's just not that simple or that fast." "Let me finish up with these gentlemen." "They're leaving in the morning for Parris Island to begin their training." The new future Marines began to laugh, point at me and to poke one another while mocking me.

Gunnery Sergeant Fitzgerald jumped to his feet and yelled. "The first thing we learn as Marines is that we take care of each other." "One day, and it may be sooner than you think, this man may be in the position to save your lives, and you his." "Start thinking like a Marine or you may just find yourselves right back in New York having failed to meet the requirements to become a member of this (pointing to his chest) special breed of men." "Now," he commanded, Pick up your paperwork, be on time in the morning," "Good luck, and get the hell out of my sight."

Each one in turn came up to me, shook my hand and wished me good-luck. They filed out on to busy Times Square. The last kid had brown hair and green eyes. Acne had taken its toll on his face but he was still kind of handsome. As he shook my hand he told me that his name was Jack. "See you in the corps buddy." It was almost three years before I would see Jack again. When next we met, I was holding what was left of his head in my hands, while his brains spilled out between my fingers. That was during a combat operation that was called Union II.

It is very strange how I remembered Jack. Our first meeting took only a few seconds. It took him almost an hour to die in my arms. Often in fitful sleep I still remember Jack. I will always remember him. "What's your name young fella?" Gunnery Sergeant Fitzgerald asked," Bobby no, Robert." I answered. "Well Bobby, no Robert. He said smiling. "This is how it's done." "First I have to give you a test in order to find out if you are qualified to become a Marine." "Then once that is determined I'll send you down to Whitehall Street for more testing and a physical." If all goes well I'll complete your paperwork which will include a document with your parent's signatures on it giving you permission to join the Marine Corps."

"I see that you can't be a day over seventeen." "So I going to need their signatures and the documents have to be notarized." "Understand?" "Yes sir," was my answer. "Let's get started sir." "I'm ready to join." I continued.

How was I going to pull this off? I had no idea. You see I was just turning fifteen years old. Gunnery Sergeant Fitzgerald gave me the test and I aced it. He said, "Son nobody has ever done this before." Do you mind if I give you another one?"

It was a different one this time. I aced that one too. "Young man let me get your ass down to Whitehall Street by 0600 hours tomorrow morning, alright?" "I've never seen any shit like this before in my life." He said. "Nobody is going to believe this mother fucking shit, "No-fuck-n-body." I smiled and thought to myself, "Welcome to Bobby's world." Gunnery Sergeant Fitzgerald gave me a brown envelope with all the papers that I would need for the next day and he gave me two subway tokens. All the way back uptown I wondered how in the world was I going to pull this off?

My desire to escape the harshness of my life was overpowering. I would find a way. The first stop was at Gut's house to tell Mrs. Gutloff what I was about to do. I begged her to sign for me but she just asked, "Have you lost your mind joining the Marines?" I took that as a no, and left. Next I went up to Mrs. Margaret's, "Have you lost your mind joining the Marines?" She asked. Another no as far as I was concerned so I didn't even bother to ask her to sign my mothers' name on the consent form.

What I did do was explain to her that this was a way out for me and that I needed her to keep this just between us. She agreed and I left after kissing her on her forehead and thanking her. There were no more options. What I would do is just go down to Whitehall Street in the morning and take it from there.

Hopes were fading fast. At three o'clock of the next morning I slid down the wall in the air shaft and made my way through the basement and up on to the street. We didn't have a slam lock. Leaving the front door unlocked would have meant death for me, when my father discovered it unlocked and me gone.

Before I left I washed very carefully with octagon soap and put baby powder all over my body. This was an attempt to make myself smell a little fresher and cleaner. It worked somewhat, but the soap made me itch something terrible.

The number one train was a local, so it made a stop at every station along the way, at the stop before South Ferry; a stop that I was very familiar with, the conductor announced that anyone wanting to exist at that stop should move to the last three cars. I followed his instructions and exited the train at the South Ferry stop. It was still dark when I came out of the station. The light of day was just showing itself in the black gray sky off in the distance coming from the east.

Young boys were exiting and walking toward Whitehall Street, two blocks across from the station. Some, I would find out later were drafted and really didn't want to be there. Others like me had enlisted and were looking forward to passing these final test and becoming Sailors, Marines, Soldiers and Airmen.

They were all so young. These boys you would have expected to see out and about on their way to a high school basketball game or to an afternoon school dance. From what I was reading in the newspaper, I came to realize that most, the draftees and those who had enlisted would in a few short months be in a place called Vietnam, a place whose name at the time meant nothing but would very soon become a part of nightly news history.

The nation would, because of live media reporting, get to see some of these young boys die on the six o'clock news. None of us, I believed then, even gave Vietnam a second thought. After all we were little boys with our whole lives ahead of us.

Names like Leach Valley and Hamburger Hill, and An Hoa, The Rockpile, did not yet exist. Nor did any of those hills that Americans named that were referred to by there height. Like 881 North and South. And Hue City was a place that none knew existed. Later the names would be remembered as some of the bloodiest battles fought in Vietnam. The roar of the rifles and the impact of the bullets would one day render some of these children forever young in the minds of old men who once dreamed the dreams that they once did before the ravishes of time found us slumped and mentally wounded as lost survivors.

I know for a fact that each and everyone who walked out of that train station that morning saw that Green Lady off in the darkness standing there in the harbor with her torch ablaze. She was our lady. A symbol of what we were as a nation and a people, a part of every one of us wanted to protect what she stood for. This I truly believed, that morning for fleeting seconds I felt that way. I was not Pissy Bobby or smart-ass motherfucker of cocksucker or bastard anymore. I was an American.

The induction center on Whitehall Street was constructed with brown sand stone. It was old and draftee. When I entered the building there was an Army Sergeant standing in the foyer directing us where we were to go. Those who were leaving and getting sworn in were motioned to the right, those testing and taking physicals to the left. There must have been two hundred or more of us in the room on the left. "Have a seat where you can find one and give me your full attention."

Those were the words of a stocky Marine Staff Sergeant. "My name is Staff Sergeant Smith." "You will follow my direction to the letter during this process." When I give you the word you will form a single line facing the door that you came in through." "There will be a Sergeant standing there who will give each one of you some forms that you will fill out as you go through this process." "Plan on being here for a while, now do it." As though as one, we moved and lined up as we were told to do.

The first thing that we did was to file up the stairs into a room with tables and chairs. Another sergeant passed out test, after more instruction we took it. Then we had our hearing tested in little booths. After the hearing test we were given a basket and a small canvas bag that we were told to hang around our necks after we had stripped necked and placed our clothes in the wire basket. The wire basket was handed to a man in a cage and we were given a little brass tag with a number on it. Then we proceeded to stand in line until directed to move forward in groups of ten so that we could be x-rayed and examined by an Army doctor.

The doctor ordered us to stand on one leg and then the other. Then as he stood in front of us he told us to cough as he applied pressure to each side if our scrotums. Then we were told to turn around. "Raise your left foot; now raise your right foot." "Bend over and touch your toes." "Good." "Now reach back and spread your cheeks." We stood like that holding our cheeks apart until the doctor had passed by. As he passed by you, the command was given for you to stand up and move toward the door. Once finished we dressed and went back down stairs to the same room that we started out in.

Staff Sergeant Smith was sitting at a desk in the middle of the room. He motioned for us to hand him our paper work and then he motioned for us to sit down. My heart was pounding so hard that I thought everyone in the room could hear it. My first step to becoming a Marine was over. "Dickerson, Robert E, Dickerson." It was Staff Sergeant Smith. "Yes Sir, that's me." I responded. "Get over here." He said. "I want you to you follow me."

We went into a small office and Staff Sergeant Smith told me to have a seat. When he started to speak my whole world came crashing down on me. "Son," he began. "I have some bad news for you." "The doctor wrote here that you have an unusual number of infected wounds on your body." "We need to know how they happened." Depending on how truthful you answer me I will decide to either send you home or to process you through so that you can become a United States Marines." "I play a lot of football sir and I don't have any equipment I…"

Before I could finish he was up in my face. "Don't lie to me son." He yelled. "Don't you want to be a Marine?" "Get out of here!" "Now move it." "Please sir, don't send me back there." "Back there where?" He asked, "Home, home to my mother and father." I said. As he was turning to face the window behind him he asked. "Did they do this to you?" I said, "Yes sir, them and others in my family." How old are you son?" He asked. I said, Sir, seventeen." He started to laugh at my response and said, "Seventeen my ass." "You lying little fuck." "You can't go back there huh?" "No sir," I said. Still laughing he told me to get the hell out of his sight and assured me that he would take care of my paperwork and process me through if I could get someone to sign the consent forms.

There was one more thing that he said as I was walking out of the room. "Marines aren't supposed to cry, wipe your eyes before you leave the room." "Don't worry," he said. "You are going to become a Marine." "I won't stand in your way if you don't let those injures stand in your way." The walk back to the train station brought to mind the issue of parental consent. Then it dawned on me, Dr. Mills was a notary.

He said he would do anything for me. It would be a lot to ask of him after all his years of support and kindness, but I had to. Would he risk everything that he had worked for and built just to help a nothing and a nobody like me? Tomorrow, I thought, above the rumble of the wheels on the tracks. I'll ask him. Walking from the train station on 125th street and Lexington I was torn between humming the "Marine Corps Hymn," because I was happy or "Nobody Knows the Trouble I've Seen," because I was afraid of what awaited me once I got home.

I had been gone all day, not having given either of my parents an explanation as to where I was going or what I would be doing. They were waiting for me. I could feel it. When I got to my building I stood on the stoop and leaned over the railing so that I could peep into the window. Pop was sitting in his chair not watching but looking through the television set. When I knocked on the door he answered. "Who in the fuck is it?" "Daddy it's me Bobby." I called out. "Well, if any body named Bobby brings his ass up in here he's a dead mother fucker." He yelled back. I turned and walked away. Then I knew that I couldn't go into that apartment. I knew that I would never again be able to go home. The die had been cast. There could be no turning back now.

I walked down the hallway and sat down under the steps and fell asleep. Tomorrow, I've been told brings its own problems. My thoughts were focused more on getting Dr. Mills to understand that this would be the only chance that I would have to get away. If he wouldn't help me I would have to endure three more years of suffering and abuse before I would be old enough to enlist without needing them to sign for me. I prayed to the God that up until this point had ignored me.

Mr. Frank, as was his habit, opened his candy store at 6:00 every morning. I was waiting outside when he arrived. It had been seventy-two hours since I had eaten anything. He wasn't one for small talk so when I said good morning he just tapped me no the shoulder and nodded. After he had pulled back the gate on the door and opened it, he invited me in. "Hungry?" He said. "Kind of," I said in response. "Boy, either you are or you're not." "No two ways about it." "Which is it?" He asked. To clear up the matter I told him that I was hungry. "C'mon up in here and I'll fix you some tea with lemon and see what else I got up in here."

The donuts and Danish were always sitting in front of the store when he arrived. Mr. Frank opened the box and gave me one jelly donut and cherry Danish. He then fixed me a cup of tea with lemon and five sugars'. He knew just what I liked. "Did somebody hurt you?" "No Mr. Frank, nobody hurt me." "Can I ask you a favor?" Mr. Frank turned and said jokingly, "Sure long as you don't ask me for no money." "If I gave you some money we couldn't be friends no mo." I half laughed and continued. "Mr. Frank, can you sign some papers for me?" He walked up to me and looking very ashamed said, "Bobby, how come everybody in the neighborhood knows that I can count but I can't read or write, and you don't?" "Oh, Mr. Frank, I'm so sorry that I offended you." "Please forgive me." I stammered, "No need for forgiveness boy," he said. "My business is money not read-n and write-n." "I count money not words."

So I ate and sipped my tea in silence even though Mr. Frank was as talkative as he was on Sunday after he had had a taste or two. When I had finished I extended my hand for Mr. Frank to shake it and told him that I was thankful for all that he had done for me over the years. Mr. Frank slapped my hand away and reached out and hugged me. "Bobby I don't know where you be going, but God bless you and take care of you."

As he spoke tears began to fall down his face. I'd never seen Mr. Frank like this before. "Go-woon bye," "Just go-woon, I'm gonna miss your help and your smile." Mr. Frank reached under the counter, pulled out a bottle. Poured some of its contents into a white Dixie cup and had a taste on Tuesday. "See ya Mr. Frank and thanks again." He gestured with a half wave, half salute, and we parted ways. While crossing to the other side of the street, Mr. Frank came out of his store and yelled for me to look in my back pocket. When I did there were two-dollar bills there. I waved and said thank you.

I felt exceptional. Mr. Frank never gave anybody anything. Not even prolonged conversation. Looking back I believe that he sensed that my life was about to change forever and his gift of two dollars was his way of saying that I was all right in his book. What I didn't I know then was that it was his way of saying good-bye to a little friend.

By the time I made my way back to his store a few years later, he wasn't there anymore. Having been helped along by his heavy drinking he had died, his liver was destroyed. Mr. Frank had fallen asleep in death. "Now there is a likely prospect." I said to myself as I caught a glimpse of Mr. Harry walking slowly across the street. All the kids who lived on our block called him Harry the Wine-O, I never did, and he was always Mr. Harry to me. Mr. Harry was very light skinned, thin and wore very thick glasses.

Mr. Saunders, one of the building superintendents on our block let him sleep in the basement and paid him a small amount for helping do things around the building. It wasn't much, just enough for Mr. Harry to buy his wine, Golden Spur, he liked it chilled. Whenever I was able I would always give him fifty cents to help him out on his lean pocket days. In turn, Mr. Harry, after about a half of a bottle, would keep me entertained in conversation about the old New York and Harlem. We would sit on the stoop or walk over to P.S. 133's schoolyard and sit on the bench and talk for as long as the bottle lasted.

When sober he moved at a snails pace and didn't utter a word. Once wined up he talked a blue streak up the side of a six-story building. Mr. Harry was a wealth of knowledge and I enjoyed his company. So investing in a bottle of wine for him might, more than likely, get me one of the signatures that I needed. "Good morning Mr. Harry!" I called out. "Mr. Harry," I called out again. He stopped and turned around searching for where the voice had come from. Straining to see and to focus in on me Mr. Harry looked over the top of his glasses then the bottom.

"Is that you Bobby?" He asked. "Sure is." "Where are you on your way to this morning, Mr. Harry?" I inquired. His face and eyes were puffy and his lips were discolored from years of drinking. His skin had a yellowish hew about it and as always he shook violently when he was in need of his wine. There was no way you could determine how old he was. The years of drinking cheap wine and eating poorly had taken a heavy toll on his body.

His age, if I were to take a guess, was forty to forty-five years old. "I'll be leaving in a couple of days Mr. Harry and I just wanted to say good bye." I told him; maybe I could do something nice for you before I leave." "Would that be alright?" I asked. Bending his head and upper body forward he peeked over the top of his dirty thick coke bottle glasses and asked, "Where you going?" "You want to do something else nice for me?" "Don't you always do nice things for me?" "What this time?" "Covers when I am cold, some change or just a nice long conversation?" "What?" As I turned him toward 128th street I said. "Come with me around the corner to Miss Tiny's house then I'll tell you where I'm going."

A wicked little smile came across his face. "Lead on my boy, lead on." He spoke, half sang. With a little more pep in his step we proceeded to go to Miss Tiny's. Miss Tiny wasn't Tiny by a long shot. Short maybe, but big. I had never seen her venture out of her apartment. I always ran errands for her. Heck, I had never seen her walk. She was always sitting in the window minding everyone else's business. She was the local bootleg sales lady. A pint bottle of cheap wine will cost fifty cents at the store. Miss Tiny charged seventy-five cent.

Late at night, holidays, Sundays and early in the morning her business boomed. Paying her inflated prices mattered not to those who needed what she stocked and sold, a bottle of this or that of comfort and happiness. The sweet or burning nectar she sold that soothed the soul, courage in a bottle, relief from ones pain, the Viagra of its day, a pinch bottle, one half of a pint, a pint or a fifth. If you could pay for it, you could get it. One's hearts desire was supplied through the window wrapped in old newspaper.

It wasn't like everybody in the world didn't know what she was doing. Even the cops knew. They just didn't bother Miss Tiny. Cops like a little taste now and then too.

Miss Tiny was a fixture in the neighborhood, so nobody cared and nobody bothered Miss Tiny. "Isn't this a lovely day?" I asked as I leaped up the five steps on her stoop. You could lean from the top of the stoop almost all the way into the window on the ground floor. "Miss Tiny I just stopped by to say good-bye and to get my friend Mr. Harry here a little something to get him through the day." "Sho as hell none of my business where you be headed, but I'll be damned to hell if-n I don't want to know." She said with snuff dripping out of the corner of her mouth.

"Is that Mr. Harry there with you?" "I know what he needs; still don't know where you are going, not that it be any of my business, but I'll be damned if-n I don't want to know." She said again. "Who gonna run my errands and such when you gone?" "Everybody knows that I don't git around, I don't git around at t'all." She said in a half whimper. I leaned over and told her that if I didn't leave I was going to die. "I need to get a paper signed by Mr. Harry and somebody else." "That way I can get into the Marines and nobody will beat or hurt me ever again."

"I'll be free Miss Tiny." I told her. "Miss Tiny said, "Give me the paper boy." "What name you need on it that will get you in the Army?" "C'mon, now, let's do this thing so I can be about my business and you can git on about yours." I showed her where to sign and told her how to spell my mothers' name, she signed it, and I was one third of the way there. Here she said, "Give this cup to Mr. Harry."

"He ain't used to the good stuff, but it'll stop those shakes faster than wine, so's he will be able to sign this here paper." Mr. Harry swallowed the contents in one gulp. "Ahhhh sure sets the sun high in the morning sky this does." Mr. Harry said. "Mr. Harry, she called out." "Get up here and write a name on this here paper." "Tell him what name to put-n- on there." Miss Tiny said in her broken form of English.

With his shakes gone Mr. Harry was able to write my fathers' name where it was supposed to go. "Mr. Harry, Miss Tiny, thank you so much." I told them. "What you need for Mr. Harry?" She asked, acting as though she hadn't heard me. "A pint of what he likes if you please." I said while handing her a dollar. She placed her hand over the dollar in my hand and closed it. "Here, sweet heart, she said while handing me a fifth bottle. "This one is on Miss Tiny," "Its gonna be a nice day for you, gonna be a long day for Mr. Harry." "Keep Yo money and may God keep you." "Take care of yourself and don't forget old Miss Tiny."

Miss Tiny, I asked. "What's your real name?" "Ain't important, son, don't nobody call me by it no way." "It's a beautiful name as I remember, ain't been called by it since I don't know when, but it don't matter now no ways." And it don't matter to me no mo, every one just calls me Miss Tiny." That's what I call a good enough name to be called by." "Yep." "Though I ain't tiny no mo, I'm just called Miss Tiny." "Now go before I cry." When I was half way down the block, consent papers in hand Mr. Harry in tow, Miss Tiny yelled. "Still don't know who'll be running my errands with you gone." "Lord, my lord, who gonna run my errands when you gone?" I didn't look back. If I had, I truly believe I would have cried.

This out pouring of support was unexpected. Now I was two thirds of the way toward freedom. The fat man who sold vegetables in Mr. Berney's Butcher shop was taking his morning delivery of crates of vegetables into the store. He no longer had any interest in me; his thing was defenseless little boys. There was no exchanging of words or glances. I just walked pass. There was no need for comments that would be expressions of disdain or contempt. Even after all that had been done to me by him, it didn't matter any more. The emotion hate still eluded me.

There was more of a feeling of sorrow for him. It was many years later when I learned that a lady had stabbed him to death one Sunday morning while he was sitting on his stool. Maybe her child told her what he had done to him, a befitting end I can't say. What I do know is that a mother thought that his actions was deserving of such an end. Even to this day I am incapable of taking on the role of being the judge.

Still, in the end, I take it as it comes. It makes my life simple. When Mr. Harry and I got in front of Dr. Mills drug store he expressed a desire to return to his bedding beside the furnace in Mr. Saunders basement. "My boy," he said. "Parting is such sweet sorrow, but part we must until tomorrow." I have an appointment with the grape and you have one with destiny, onward my gallant lad, onward." Then becoming more serious he said, "Thank you for always being a gentleman. "I bid you a safe venture into life and a fond farewell." Then he walked hurriedly across the street and down 129th street.

When he arrived at Mr. Saunders building he took out the fifth of wine from under his jacket. Raised it, and called out, "To a friend." After taking a swig he vanished down the steps leading to the basement. A little over a year after,

Mr. Harry was found dead wrapped in a blanket beside the furnace where he slept with the remains of a pint of Golden Spur wine by his side. He had been dead for some time. The wine was no longer chilled, as he liked it.

Sadly, I found out, there was no grave that I could visit. No head stone that marked where he lay. The city of New York had disposed of his remains without ceremony on Hearts Island, Potter's Field. Mr. Harry was my friend and I will never forget him. I visit him often where he is buried in my heart. Dr. Mills was already inside but had not opened yet. I knocked on the door and after looking through the shade that covered it he opened the door for me.

"Come on in Son." He invited, "What's wrong, what can I do for you?" "You hungry, are you hurt?" He questioned. "No, Dr. Mills, I'm not hungry, I ate over at Mr. Franks this morning." "I do need you to help me though." "You know how things have been for me over the years." "I have a chance to get away. "A chance to go somewhere where nobody will ever again call me names or beat me." "Say that you will help me this one last time." I begged. Dr. Mills told me to come behind the counter and roll up my shirtsleeves and pants legs. "Sit down Son." He instructed as he took down a box of cotton and the bottle of the solution that he always used to clean up my sores.

"This sounds pretty important." "Let's take it slow and I'll see what I can do for you." He said as he wiped and cleaned my infected wounds. Dr. Mills I've gotten two people to sign my parents name to a consent form so that I can join the Marines." "What I would like you to do is notarize it for me and I can leave in a couple of days." I was able to say all of that in between the winces. The solution always burned when it made contact with my wounds.

Dr. Mills stood up and walked over to his desk and opened a drawer. He removed a black leather box about six inches long, four inches wide and four inches deep. The box was placed un-opened on the table next to me. "You know that if I do what you ask I could lose everything that I have worked for?" He asked. "What I must do at this point is abandon my morals, depart from all that is honorable and just in a commission granted me by the State of New York." Honor and integrity, Bobby, is what I have always seen in you, and now you ask me to do this thing for you."

Dr. Mills seemed torn and broken as he spoke those words. Rising to my feet I told him that I was sorry and turned to leave. Before I had taken four steps he rushed up to me cradled me in his arms. He said, "This time, my boy, I must commit a wrong for the better good." "Give me the paper." I fumbled as I removed it from my back pocket and handed it to him. Dr. Mills stamped his seal of notary on the consent form and signed it. "When you complete your training, son, come back so that I can see you in your uniform." Now go and be better than what you have been made to believe that you are." "Become a Marine son; make me proud of what I have done." "When you think of me, sing a little song for me."

He walked me to the door and opened it. Then he said, "Today you are a young man, so, rather than hug you, I would like the honor of being the first to shake the hand of a Marine." I extended my hand and thanked him. He grabbed mine with both of his and shook it. I saw him start to cry out of the corner of my eye as I walked away.

Here mortal man had done more for me than a God that I talked to all the time had done. This mortal man gave me a means of escaping the pain and brutal torment of my everyday life. He freed me with a rubber stamp and the stroke of a pen. I started my long walk down to see Gunnery Sergeant Fitzgerald at his office on Times Square. When I arrived he was very glad to see me, and showed a great deal of delight when I handed him my consent form along with the rest of my paperwork. "When do you want to leave boot (boot is a term used by the Marine Corps to describe a basic Marine)?" He asked. "Now sir if possible," I said. "How about I get you out of here the day after tomorrow, good enough?" He said smiling. "Yes Sir, I'll be ready." "Day after tomorrow, I'll be there." I gushed out.

Gunnery Sergeant Fitzgerald explained the process to me. First thing the day after tomorrow

I had to report to Whitehall Street by six o'clock in the morning. Once there they would complete the process and I would be sworn into the United States Marine Corps. After we were fed our last civilian meal we would board a bus to Newark airport where we would be flown to Charleston South Carolina. Then we would be taken to Paris Island where we would begin eight weeks of the most intense training in the United States Military.

"Here's your paperwork boot, welcome to the United States Marine Corps." "Good luck," he said. Sadly the Gunny never got the chance to see me as a full-fledged Marine. In 1968 he was killed in Vietnam in a place called Hue City. His body was returned to the states and to his family with a tag on it that read, Remains non-viewable. With nowhere to go that night I used the token that the Gunnery Sergeant had given me to gain access to the subway.

That evening, and all the next day and night, I rode uptown and downtown. Into Brooklyn, all over wherever the train could take me. When possible I got a few hours of sleep and washed in the bathrooms at the different stops along the way. Not having enough money to re-enter the subway once I had existed. I never got the chance to say good-bye to Mrs. Margaret or Mrs. Gutloff. Returning to the neighborhood would have brought me too close to my family. I didn't want to encounter them walking down the street or entering the building to visit Mrs. Margaret.

Simply put, with only a few hours before my departure it wasn't worth the chance. I never saw Mrs. Margaret alive again. When next I saw Vivian, Mrs. Margaret had passed away.

The risk was not greater than the reward. During my final hours before I left New York to start training in Marine boot camp. My only concern was what if I wet the bed? It was my understanding that wetting the bed was grounds for discharge. Here I was fifteen years old on my way to Paris Island and I still wet the bed. Failure was written all over my desires to find a place to belong and freedom from abuse, for me, for the rest of my life. Failure could not be an option. Failure meant returning to this hellhole of a life.

When I arrived at the South Ferry station on the morning of my departure, it was around five thirty. Rather than go directly to the induction center I paused to gaze out over the black waters of the East River. The soft splashing sounds that the waves made breaking against the wall below me lulled me into a recounting of old vivid memories of my past. All of the beatings, starvations and verbal abuse flashed in a kaleidoscope of bright colors in my mind.

I wondered if my parents were looking for me, if they missed me, or if they thought that I was at last dead and out of their hair once and for all. For the first time in my life the reality of my lonely existence caused me to break down emotionally. Sobbing uncontrollably I fought to pull myself together. Once composed, I turned way from the blackness of the river and walked across the street and into the room on the right.

Staff Sergeant Smith was sitting at a desk against the wall. We were the only two in the room at the time. When he looked up and saw me he winked and said, "I see you made it." "Have a seat we'll get this show on the road when the rest arrive." The room soon began to fill with young boys of all shapes, sizes and colors from all over New York City.

A baby faced Marine entered the room told all those who were enlisting in the Marines to form a single line against the left wall with their paperwork in their right hands. About thirty of us complied. "Somebody will be with you people in a Moment." He barked. Then he made his exit through the door by which he had entered. We stood there for what seemed like an hour before the same Marine came back in and told us to follow him single file into another room.

As we entered we were lined up in rows of five, one row behind the other. There was an American flag at our front and a podium. Another three quarters of an hour passed before Staff Smith, the baby faced Marine and an Army Major entered the room. "Pay attention people, listen up," roared the young Marine. The Major started to speak, "Once you raise your right hands and take this oath you will be a basic Marine in the United States Marine Corps." "You will be subject to the rules and regulations as set forth in the Uniform Code of Military Justice."

"Once sworn in, if you leave an area to which you have been assigned without being told to, you-will-be charged with A.W.O.L." If you fail to be accounted for at your designated point of departure, I assure you that you will be hunted down, arrested and charged with desertion." "Now raise your right hand and repeat after me."

We all took the oath and became members of the most elite fighting service in the world. At last, I thought, I belong. At two o'clock we were given a lunch that included a ham and cheese sandwich, a small container of Luke warm milk, and an apple. We were then told to fall outside, line up to the left of the main entrance of the building take ten and light em! And smoke em! If you got em! "Don't take all day ladies." "The bus will be here in a few to take you to the airport." Information again imparted on us by the baby face Marine.

The buses arrived as promised and we boarded single file and took our seats. All the way up town the rest of the guys sang the Marine Corps hymn over and over, until we started to drive across the George Washington Bridge. The bus became silent. They, I assumed, realized that this was the last time any of them would see home for the next four months. The next sound was the voice of the young Marine telling us to file off of the bus and go directly into the airport terminal. "You, buddy, come here." The young Marine was calling me. "Yes Sir." I responded.

"You're going to be in charge of the group

until you arrive at your destination, Paris Island Receiving." "At that time you will, private, will hand these documents over to the Sergeant that will warmly greet you upon your arrival." "I hope that I have made myself clear?" "Yes Sir, will do." I responded in my best John Wayne Marine voice. "Carry on." "What's your name?" "Dickerson, sir," I told him, "Well Dickerson." "My name is Corporal Austin." "If you fuck this up and not do exactly as I told you, I will make a call to your Drill Instructor on the island." "Trust me; your stay on Parris Island will be the most educational time of your life if you fail." "You get my drift?"

Not knowing what to say I just nodded my head up and down. "He said that it was good that we had come to an understanding and escorted us to our boarding gate, we boarded and soon were airborne. Looking out of the airplane window I saw the north disappear under the clouds as the plane banked south. When we landed in Charleston South Carolina it was dark. We boarded a green bus with U.S. Marines stenciled in yellow paint on either side of the hood.

A spit and polished Marine was driving. His uniform had the sharpest creases that I had ever seen before. "Is everybody comfortable?" "Ok then, we are on our way." He yelled back to us. Then he pulled away. The kid sitting next to me mentioned how nice he was, and said that he was looking forward to boot camp and getting his uniforms, I just smiled as he continued talking for the next hour.

The bus crossed the bridge and stopped at the main gate that was painted red. In bold gold letters were the words, "Parris Island U.S. Marine Corps Recruit Depot." "Welcome." Well, I thought, this is it. I'm really going to be a Marine. From this moment on I never have to worry about being abused or beaten again.

Never before in my life, had I been anywhere that was as dark as Parris Island. The night was absolutely black except for a light over a sign that read, "Receiving Barracks," there were rows of yellow footprints in front of the Barracks and I barely made out the shape of the three men in uniform standing at Parade rest.

The most noticeable thing about them was their Smokey the Bear hats. The door of the bus was opened by the driver and one of the Marines that was standing there in front of the barracks ran onto the bus yelling, "Get the fuck off my bus and fall in on the yellow footprints outside." "Move maggots move." The other two joined in "You stupid fuck, don't you know what a foot print is?" "Go ahead hog, just fall the fuck down." "Get up." "Get off my god damn bus." "Line the fuck up." "Shut up."

Everybody was confused and was tripping all over each other. When I stepped down off of the bus I walked over to one of the Drill Instructors and introduced myself. "Sir my name is Robert E. Dickerson and I am in charge of these men and their paperwork." "In charge, in charge of what, hog?" "You scum sucking homesick, shit for brains maggot." "You ain't even in charge of your own ass, I am!" All the time he was yelling at me he was hitting me in the forehead with the brim of his hat.

"Sir I was told to give this paperwork to you." I said handing him the package that contained all of our paperwork. "Are you stupid?" "Did anybody tell you open your shit hole and speak?" "Did you call me a fucking you?" All this he was able to say in one breath. "A you is a female sheep." "Do I look like a female sheep, pig?" "You like fucking sheep?" "You want to fuck me Priv?" I think in response I managed to say, "Yes, No, No, Yes," before he grabbed me around my neck. While calling me commie motherfucker, shit for brains, maggot and hog, then just like it was back home, he kicked and beat me.

Bobby

The dawn is here and still I have not come in from the night. The dawn has shown me that there is nothing bigger, nothing better out there for me. I searched for it, but never found it. If there were something bigger and better out there I would have found some peace. I, in fact, have for years tried hard to stop tomorrow from coming, just hanging on to yesterday. That is what I find myself doing, that is what, I believe, we all do. What I want to leave with you is this. Everyday when you wake up, tell each other that you love one-another. Say it and mean it from the heart.

There, I have given you the greatest gift any human could possibly give to another, Love. There in, the breaking of the new dawn, you will find the bigger and better that was lost to me. In the new dawn of tomorrow you will find a welcoming and a way to forget the old pains of yesterday. Then and only then will you come to realize that the peace that you sought for so long was right there inside of you all the time.

Perhaps my passing through your time and space, will, I hope have given you some peace. As, for me, well, I will be lost in time, but maybe I'll find my eternity in one of you. The world is a beautiful, clear, pool of refreshing water. Drink, you must, as much of its beauty as you are able, everyday. And from it feed the thirst of others. Like it or not, I have changed the world, just by leaving my footprints upon it. I have dampened its soil with my tears, and my blood has poured out on its green grasses. Now in the twilight of my time I will go back into it, my world, and become what I was before I was Bobby, Nothing.

Sadness

His name is Mr. Michael Dickerson and he and his Lady, Ms. Candice has blessed me with a beautiful grand daughter. The little Princess is named Raine. I only wish that he and I could be friends. He is my son, but I will never be his father. Oh, what tender dreams have the little one's dreamed, that we as parents have not torn apart? Revenge is a dish best served cold.

For a Simple Friendship and Moments of Peace

Ms. Jo' lle

Rest in Eternal Peace

Aunt Mattie T. Bailey

April 2007

I will never forget your unconditional love. We are all Angels with one wing. How can I fly without you? The day that you left me I fell from the sky.